From Human-Centered Design to Human-Centered Society

A human-centered society creatively balances investments in sources of innovation, while also governing in a manner that eventually limits exploitation by originators once innovations have proven their value in the marketplace, broadly defined to include both private and public constituencies.

The desired balance requires society to invest in constituencies to be able to create innovations that provide current and future collective benefits, while also assuring society provides laws, courts, police, and military to protect individual rights to life, liberty, and the pursuit of happiness.

The balance addresses collectivism vs. individualism. Collectivism emphasizes the importance of the community. Individualism, in contrast, is focused on the rights and concerns of each person. Unity and selflessness or altruism are valued traits in collectivist cultures; independence and personal identity are central in individualistic cultures.

Collectivists can become so focused on collective benefits that they ignore sources and opportunities for innovation. Individualists can tend to invest themselves, almost irrationally, in ideas and visions, many of which will fail, but some will transform society. Collectivists need to let individualists exploit their successful ideas. Individualists need to eventually accept the need to provide collective benefits.

This book addresses the inherent tension underlying the pursuit of this balance. It has played a central role in society at least since the Industrial Revolution (1760–1840). Thus, the story of this tension, how it regularly emerges, and how it is repeatedly resolved, for better or worse, is almost a couple of centuries old. Creating a human-centered society can be enabled by creatively enabling this balance. Explicitly recognizing the need for this balance is a key success factor.

This book draws upon extensive experiences within the domains of transportation and defense, computing and communications, the Internet and social media, health and wellness, and energy and climate. Balancing innovation and exploitation takes varying forms in these different domains. Nevertheless, the underlying patterns and practices are sufficiently similar to enable important generalizations.

From Human-Centered Design to Human-Centered Society

Creatively Balancing Business Innovation and Societal Exploitation

William B. Rouse

Routledge
Taylor & Francis Group

A PRODUCTIVITY PRESS BOOK

First published 2024
by Routledge
605 Third Avenue, New York, NY 10158

and by Routledge
4 Park Square, Milton Park, Abingdon, Oxon, OX14 4RN

Routledge is an imprint of the Taylor & Francis Group, an informa business

ISBN: 978-1-032-61174-7 (hbk)
ISBN: 978-1-032-61173-0 (pbk)
ISBN: 978-1-003-46236-1 (ebk)

DOI: 10.4324/9781003462361

Typeset in Minion
by Deanta Global Publishing Services, Chennai, India

Contents

Preface

I have been formulating, applying, and extending human-centered design for over four decades. At first, I applied this philosophy and methodology to airplanes, automobiles, factories, power plants, and ships. Key stakeholders in these endeavors were operators, maintainers, managers, and designers.

More recently, over two decades, I have pursued healthcare, education, energy, and defense. Operators, maintainers, managers, and designers are still central stakeholders, but additional people of great importance range from executives, politicians, and policymakers, to teachers, students, and parents.

In all of these endeavors, human-centered design was central to creating human-centered systems. In recent years, it has struck me that pervasive human-centered systems would culminate in a human-centered society. What does that mean and how can we bring it about? Answering this question is the objective of this book.

This question can seem rather abstract until one considers it in a context. Innovation has long been a context of interest to me. I have also been interested in how innovation can lead to exploitation in terms of monopolies, worker mistreatment, and environmental impacts. Can we have the economic benefits of innovation while mitigating the impacts of exploitation?

I think we can, but we have to modify the rules of the game in our society. Innovators can still be exploiters, but only for limited windows of time. Exploitive practices have to morph into broad social benefits for everyone. This is not a novel idea. For example, patents have limited durations. However, explicitly planned and managed transitions from exploitation to broad benefits are needed to smooth practices and increase success.

This book draws upon extensive experiences with the domains of transportation and defense, computing and communications, Internet and social media, health and wellness, and energy and climate. Balancing innovation and exploitation takes varying forms in these different domains. Nevertheless, the underlying patterns and practices are sufficiently similar to enable important generalizations.

William B. Rouse
Washington, DC
July 2023

About the Author

William B. Rouse is Research Professor in the McCourt School of Public Policy at Georgetown University and Professor Emeritus and former Chair of the School of Industrial and Systems Engineering at Georgia Institute of Technology. His research focuses on mathematical and computational modeling for policy design and analysis in complex public-private ecosystems, with particular emphasis on healthcare, education, energy, transportation, and national security. He is a member of the US National Academy of Engineering and Fellow of IEEE, INCOSE, INFORMS, and HFES. His recent books include *Beyond Quick Fixes* (Oxford, 2023), *Bigger Pictures for Innovation* (Routledge, 2023), *Transforming Public-Private Ecosystems* (Oxford, 2022), *Failure Management* (Oxford, 2021), and *Computing Possible Futures* (Oxford, 2019). He lives in Washington, DC, in the United States.

1

A Central Tension

INTRODUCTION

In *Beyond Quick Fixes* (Rouse, 2023), I argued that our societal ecosystems should be human-centered. In this chapter, I explain, in detail, what that means. In this book, I articulate an integrated vision and plans for achieving this.

A human-centered society creatively balances investments in sources of innovation, while also governing in a manner that eventually limits exploitation by originators once innovations have proven their value in the marketplace, broadly defined to include both private and public constituencies.

The desired balance requires society to invest in constituencies to be able to create innovations that provide current and future collective benefits, while also assuring society provides laws, courts, police, and military to protect individual rights to life, liberty, and pursuit of happiness

The balance addresses collectivism vs. individualism. Collectivism emphasizes the importance of the community. Individualism, in contrast, is focused on the rights and concerns of each person. Unity and selflessness or altruism are valued traits in collectivist cultures; independence and personal identity are central in individualistic cultures.

Collectivists can become so focused on collective benefits that they ignore sources and opportunities for innovation. Individualists can invest themselves, almost irrationally, in ideas and visions, many of which will fail, but some will transform society. Collectivists need to let individualists exploit their successful ideas. Individualists need to eventually accept the need to provide collective benefits.

DOI: 10.4324/9781003462361-1

This book addresses the inherent tension underlying the pursuit of this balance. It has played a central role in society at least since the Industrial Revolution (1760–1840). Thus, the story of this tension, how it regularly emerges, and how it is repeatedly resolved, for better or worse, is at least a couple of centuries old. Creating a human-centered society can be enabled by creatively achieving this balance. Explicit recognition of the need for this balance is a key success factor.

EVOLUTION OF HUMAN-CENTERED SYSTEMS

Throughout my career, human-centered design has been central to creating human-centered systems. In recent years, it has struck me that pervasive human-centered systems would culminate in a human-centered society. What does that mean and how can we bring it about? Answering this question is the objective of this book.

Society has long been concerned with the well-being of people. As early as the fifth century BCE, research into the causes of illness was pursued. Hippocrates, often characterized as the father of medicine, was active in the fourth and third centuries BCE. The health of miners in ancient Greece was of particular concern.

The discipline of occupational medicine can be dated to the Italian Bernardino Ramazzini (1633–1714). His *Diseases of Workers* was published in Modena in 1700 in which he described the effects of work on health for many professions. It was published in English in 1760.

Willem Wundt (1832–1920) has been characterized as the father of experimental psychology. His book *Principles of Physiological Psychology* was published in 1874 in Leipzig, Germany. It was published in English in 1904.

Wundt (1904) and experimental psychology provide the bridge to human factors and ergonomics. William James and Sigmund Freud were also luminaries in psychology but with much less emphasis on scientific measurements. My experience has been that human factors and ergonomics in departments of psychology are typically housed in experimental psychology sections.

World War II led to greatly increased research on human abilities, limitations, and preferences as the functioning of military systems depended on such understanding. The Institute of Ergonomics and Human Factors was founded in London in 1946. The Human Factors and Ergonomics Society was founded in the US in 1957 and is the world's largest scientific association for human factors/ergonomics professionals.

Salvendy and Karwowski (2021) edited a 1,600-page *Handbook of Human Factors and Ergonomics* (5th Edition) that provides the principles, methods, and tools of human factors and ergonomics. I contributed a chapter to each edition of this handbook, beginning with the first edition in 1987. Norman (2013) provides many easily digestible illustrations of the benefits of human factors. His latest book outlines how these benefits expand to society broadly (Norman, 2023).

Human-Machine Systems

The notion of human-machine systems soon emerged (Sheridan & Ferrell, 1974; Sheridan, 1985). The essence of the idea is that humans and machines interact to perform work. We pursue an understanding of these interactions to devise means for improving work performance.

At first, this endeavor focused on people's abilities to read, reach, and lift things. The idea was to fit people into aircraft and automobile cockpits, for example. Next, we extended engineering models of machines to include equations for humans. We assumed that humans conformed to task requirements subject to constraints such as reaction times, neuromotor lags, and observation noise.

This worked rather well until we considered decision-making and problem-solving tasks where humans had much more discretion to sometimes behave in unpredictable ways. The use of computer-based decision support systems and problem-solving aids further complicated modeling of human behavior. Our predictions were inherently less precise.

Another level of complexity emerged when the focus shifted to humans monitoring and supervising automation. Sheridan (1992, 2022) extended the human-machine systems paradigm to include supervisory control. This inevitably led to the need to address who – human or computer – should be in charge and under what circumstances. Continuing developments in artificial intelligence complicate this question (Rouse & Spohrer, 2018; NAP, 2021; Shneiderman, 2022).

Human Systems Integration

Human-related issues in complex systems are not limited to human-machine interaction concerns. Once all the jobs are engineered well, how are overall personnel needs met? How does one recruit, select, and train all the people needed to perform these jobs, for example, across several million military personnel? The US Army created the MANPRINT program to address manpower and personnel integration. This represented an Army-specific approach to the overall topic of human systems integration.

Over the 1980–2010 period, the National Academies' Human Factors Committee morphed to become the Committee on Human Systems Integration. I chaired this committee in the mid-1990s. The Board on Human Systems Integration, a standing board of the National Academies was formed in 2010. The broader behavioral and social science community has endorsed this view as evidenced by the *APA Handbook of Human Systems Integration* (Boehm-Davis, Durso & Lee, 2015).

Harold Booher's leadership of MANPRINT initiated this transformation. He edited two extensive handbooks, *MANPRINT: An Approach to Systems Integration* in 1990 and *Handbook of Human Systems Integration* in 2003. I contributed chapters on human error, training and aiding, and competitiveness to the first volume, and chapters on cost/benefit analysis and new product development to the second volume.

I also contributed a chapter on the economics of human systems integration to the *APA Handbook of Human Systems Integration*. My book *The Economics of Human Systems Integration* (Rouse, 2010) addressed the valuation of investments in peoples' training and education, safety and health, and work productivity, broadly defined. A key finding was that such investments can often be justified if the organizational entity making the investments also gains the returns on investments, e.g., cost savings. Otherwise, the investing entity sees the expenditure as a cost and tries to minimize it.

Human-Centered Design

Human-centered design addresses the values, concerns, and perceptions of all stakeholders in designing, developing, deploying, and employing products, services, and policies. The basic idea is to delight primary stakeholders and gain the support of the secondary stakeholders.

This notion first occurred to me at a workshop in the late 1980s at the NASA Langley Research Center near Hampton, Virginia. Many participants were discussing pilot-centered design that focused on enhancing aircraft pilots' abilities, overcoming pilots' limitations, and fostering pilots' acceptance. I suggested that we should do this for all the human stakeholders involved in the success of an aircraft program. People asked what I specifically meant.

I responded, "Pilots may fly them, but they don't build them or buy them!"

In other words, pilots being supportive of design choices may be necessary for success, but it is not sufficient. The airlines have to want to buy the airplanes, the aerospace companies have to be willing to produce them, and regulatory bodies have to certify the use of the planes. The buyers, builders, and regulators have criteria beyond those important to pilots.

I elaborated on the human-centered design construct and an associated methodology in a book, *Design for Success* (Rouse, 1991). Two other books soon followed (Rouse, 1992, 1993), addressing innovation and organizational change. The human-centered design methodology has been applied many times and continually refined (Rouse, 2007, 2015, 2019, 2022).

The premise of human-centered design is that the major stakeholders need to perceive policies, products, and services to be valid, acceptable, and viable. Valid products, services, and policies demonstrably help solve the problems for which they are intended. Acceptable products, services, and policies solve problems in ways that stakeholders prefer. Viable products, services, and policies provide benefits that are worth the costs of use. Costs here include the efforts needed to learn and use products, services, and policies, not just the purchase price.

The overall human-centered design methodology is intended to increase validity, acceptability, and viability beyond that usually experienced with the ways in which problems of the scope addressed in this book are often pursued. This begs the question of what shortcomings plague existing approaches.

First and foremost are viability issues. Sponsors of change initiatives complain that they take too long and are too expensive. This is due in part to the business processes of sponsors. However, more fundamentally, much time and money goes into developing aspects of policies that, at least in retrospect, were not needed to address the questions of primary interest.

Second, are acceptability issues. Many key stakeholders in the types of challenges addressed in this book are not educated in analytic methods and tools. Nevertheless, they are often highly talented, have considerable influence, and will not accept that the optimal policy, somehow magically produced, is X equals 12. We need methods and tools that are more engaging for these types of stakeholders (Rouse, 2014a).

Third are validity issues. There is often concern that overall analyses are of questionable validity (Rouse, 2015, 2019, 2021, 2022). This concern is due in part to the possibility that assumptions are inconsistent across component analyses. There is also the issue of incompatible definitions of organizational states across component analyses, which can lead to misleading or incorrect results. This is particularly plaguing when one is unaware of these incompatibilities.

The overall human-centered approach overcomes these issues in several ways. The early steps of the methodology focus on problem formulation, with particular emphasis on interactive pruning of the problem space prior to any in-depth explorations. In-depth analyses tend to be expensive, so it is important to be sure they are warranted.

Second, we have found that key stakeholders value being immersed in interactive visualizations of the phenomena, and relationships among phenomena associated with their domain and the questions of interest. This enables them to manipulate controls and explore responses. This is typically done in a group setting with much discussion and debate.

Third, the overall approach explicitly addresses agreeing on a consistent set of assumptions across analyses. This prompts delving into the underpinnings of each type of analysis. The overarching question is whether connecting multiple types of analysis will yield results that are valid in the context of the questions at hand.

Human-Centered Systems

In *Beyond Quick Fixes* (Rouse, 2023) I considered how human-centered interventions could mitigate challenges in the health, education, energy, and mis/dis information ecosystems. I explored how these ecosystems could benefit from seeing them as human-centered systems. This led to my postulating how all four challenges could be mitigated as a whole, reflecting an overall human-centered society.

What if we could foster a social movement such that society's zeitgeist – defining spirit or mood – was human-centered? Might a social movement be possible? What would be required for success? To begin, we need to characterize social movements. A social movement is a loosely organized effort by a large group of people to achieve a particular goal, typically a social or political one.

Consider examples of movements targeted at just health, education, or energy. Hoffman (2003) chronicles healthcare reform and social movements in the United States. "Because of the importance of grassroots social movements, or "change from below," in the history of US reform, the relationship between social movements and demands for universal healthcare is a critical one.

National health reform campaigns in the twentieth century were initiated and run by those more concerned with defending against attacks from interest groups rather than with popular mobilization. Consequently, change was focused on immediate and incremental changes rather than transforming the healthcare system itself. However, grassroots demands have also contained the seeds of a wider critique of the American healthcare system.

Van Heertum and Torres (2011) consider changes in the US educational system over the past 30 years. They argue that neoliberalism has dominated the debate, moving away from the progressive reforms of the 60s and 70s, and making economic imperatives the key focus of schooling in America. Major trends include accountability and standards, privatization and school choice, professionalism and accreditation, resegregation and the persistence of racial achievement gaps, and the changing nature of educational research.

Hess (2018) considers social movements and energy in democracies. "Industrial transition movements emerge when there is resistance from incumbent organizations, such as large utility companies in the electricity industry, to grassroots efforts to change the industry." He analyzes the "relations among the state, industry, civil society, and social movements that provide insights into causal mechanisms in the effects of social movements on industrial transitions and energy democracy."

Notable achievements in broader arenas have included the Abolitionist Movement (1830–1870), the Women's Suffrage Movement (1848–1917), the Progressive Movement (1897–1920), and the Civil Rights Movement (1875–1968). Such social movements have taken decades to secure the outcomes sought. Many, probably most, initiatives never gain recognition as "movements." However, some do succeed, with enormous social, political, and economic consequences.

The elements of the human-centered systems movement are summarized in Figure 1.1. The central premise is that everybody wants our societal systems to perform well for everybody. This requires, of course, that we design and operate these functions as systems rather than as a patchwork of activities.

It seems reasonable to assume that we all want service systems that are efficient and effective, e.g., for health, education, energy, and information (Bossidy & Charan, 2009). While the lack of efficiency and effectiveness can result in greater profits for providers, for example, in the health system, the human-centered systems movement will find this totally unacceptable.

We should desire integration across service systems to foster synergies across public and private providers (Rouse, 2022). This integration can be technological and procedural and does not require actual mergers of organizations. The human-centered systems movement will argue and lobby for policy frameworks that encourage this form of integration.

FIGURE 1.1
Elements of a human-centered system's movement

Equitable and affordable access to services should be assured (Khanna, 2022). This requires the availability of requisite technologies and possibly subsidized access. The human-centered systems movement will foster knowledgeable access to and use of resources that will enable well-informed choices among health, education, energy, and information services.

Continuous learning and improvement of efficiency and effectiveness are central (Deming, 1982). Pursuit of the above three aspirations will result in enormous data sets that can inform improvements in efficiency and effectiveness, for instance, in terms of identifying and remediating usability issues and hindrances of critical importance to the human-centered systems movement.

We need to leverage lessons learned broadly across health, education, energy, and information services, both in the US and globally, e.g., Estonia (Heller, 2017). Inevitably, some ideas will work well and others will not. Some will only work under particular circumstances. The human-centered systems movement will work to ensure that the overall learning system explores and exploits innovations broadly.

CENTRAL ECONOMIC DEBATES

There are three long-standing debates in economics that fundamentally affect how one views the central tension in this book and how it can best be addressed. The two sides of the first debate are often associated with Friedrich Hayek and Milton Friedman on one side and John Maynard Keynes and Karl Polanyi on the other. Wapshott (2011) and Delong (2022) elaborate on this debate in considerable detail.

Succinctly, is economic growth driven by market forces or government planning? Hayek and Friedman argue that market forces determine everything and government should stay out of the way. Keynes (1936) and Polanyi (1944) counter that market forces are important, but can sometimes result in disruptive outcomes, like discrimination and unemployment, that markets are unwilling to address. Government needs to stabilize situations such as the Great Depression (1929–39) and Great Recession (2007–2009), as well as recent epidemics of AIDS, opioids, and the coronavirus.

Those touting the market economy argue that governments are terrible at picking winners and should let the marketplace enable winners to emerge through competitive forces. This does not always work, as demonstrated by the recently experienced real estate bubble (Lewis, 2011; Blinder, 2013).

In real estate mortgage markets, impenetrable derivative securities were bought and sold. The valuations and ratings of these securities were premised on any single mortgage default being a random event. In other words, the default of any particular mortgage was assumed to have no impact on the possible default of any other mortgage.

The growing demand for these securities pressured mortgage companies to lower the standards for these loans. Easily available mortgages drove the sales of homes, steadily increasing home prices. Loans with initial periods of low, or even zero, interest attracted homebuyers to adjustable-rate mortgages. Many of these people could not possibly make the mortgage payments when the rates were adjusted after the initial period.

This was of less concern than one might think because people expected to flip these houses by selling them quickly at significantly increased prices. This worked as long as prices continued increasing, but as more and more lower-quality mortgages were sold, the number of defaults increased and dampened the increasing prices, which led to further increases in defaults. The bubble quickly burst.

The defaults were not random events as assumed by those valuing these securities. They constituted what is termed a "common mode failure" where a common cause results in widespread failure. Thus, these securities were much more risky than sellers had advertised. The consequences of such misinformation were enormous.

Hayek would argue that risk-takers should earn rewards, but investment banks were not taking risks; they were selling risks that neither they nor the buyers understood. When the bubble burst, the banks and investment companies were bailed out by the government, with banks using some of this money to provide executive bonuses. Millions of homeowners lost their homes when they could not make increasing mortgage payments on homes that were now worth less than the mortgage.

Greed of investment companies and consumers buying houses they could not afford, because they intended to flip them, drove the bubble. Many understood what was happening and sold short these toxic assets. Michael Lewis in *The Big Short* notes that many of the smartest people were betting against the country. The market economy undermined the economy.

The implications for addressing the central tension are quite clear. Profit seekers are often quite willing to manipulate the rules of the game to satisfy their greedy aspirations. The changes to the health, education, and energy ecosystems that I recommend in later chapters will threaten profits. Limits on misinformation and disinformation will affect both profits and votes. I do not think that the marketplace will simply support and adapt to such changes. The government will have to play a central role, perhaps facilitating rather than regulating, but nevertheless being active.

The second debate among economists concerns sources of innovation and economic growth. Mokyr (1992) argues and illustrates how technology has long been the driver. There seems, however, to be an emerging consensus that the US leadership in innovation has waned. Gordon (2016) has argued that 1870–1970 was the United States' century of innovation. I made the same argument, based on the same line of reasoning, a couple of years earlier (Rouse, 2014b).

More recently, DeLong (2022) proposed 1870–2007 as the country's "long century" of innovation, ending with the onset of the Great Recession. The rationale for 1970 as the end point is that social networking is not as compelling as electricity and indoor plumbing. Which one would you be willing to give up? On the other hand, social media has been a compelling source of disruption.

The relevance of this debate concerns the extent to which technologies will mitigate the many challenges we face. I sense that many existing technologies, if appropriately deployed and supported, can be leveraged to address these challenges. The hurdles are much more organizational and social than technological. Overcoming these hurdles involves thoughtful planning, execution, and learning in various domains, as discussed in later chapters.

The third debate concerns a central question. Might humans be inclined to pursue the creation of a human-centered society? Would they be inherently inclined to advocate and pursue collectivist benefits to society? Or, would their inclinations be to pursue maximal individualistic benefits for themselves? Answers to these questions depend on whether one adopts the perspectives of Hobbes or Rousseau.

The English philosopher Thomas Hobbes (1588–1679) believed that humans have no moral compass unless there are predetermined rules to say what actions are good or bad. There is no morality in the state of nature. There is no social contract without an absolute power to enforce it. Therefore, justice only comes into existence when this authority is established.

Swiss philosopher Jean-Jacques Rousseau (1712–1778) defined human beings as distinct from other sentient beings by virtue of two essential characteristics, which are already present in the state of nature: human freedom and perfectibility. Humans have two traits in common with other animals: the self-preservation instinct; and empathy for the rest of one's species, both of which precede reason and sociability.

Consider several scientific studies of human nature, drawing upon psychology rather than philosophy, although all of them cite the Hobbes vs. Rousseau contrast. Jarrett (2018) summarizes ten findings in psychology that clearly support the views of Hobbes rather than Rousseau. We are inherently selfish but we can possibly will ourselves beyond these inclinations.

Wrangham (2019) observes that "There is plenty of evidence that humans have innate tendencies for kindness, just as there is for our having spontaneously selfish feelings that can lead to aggression. The Hobbes-Rousseau debate is "less about biology or psychology and more about social causes, political structures, and the moral high ground." He notes that matriarchal societies tend to be less aggressive than patriarchal societies.

Ward (2012) reports that "In every single study, faster – that is, more intuitive – decisions were associated with higher levels of cooperation, whereas slower – that is, more reflective – decisions were associated with higher levels of selfishness." He also observes that "Cooperation is the intuitive response only for those who routinely engage in interactions where this behavior is rewarded – that human 'goodness' may result from the acquisition of a regularly rewarded trait."

Van Lange (2019) indicates that

> The goodness of humankind occurs most often between two people. We are naturally kind toward another person. Empathy and reciprocity rapidly do their work. Empathy is an emotion that is especially activated by a single individual, not a group of other people. Reciprocity is easy in pairs, but more challenging in groups of three or more.

> The badness of humankind occurs most often between groups of people. When individuals are part of groups, things are much more likely to go

wrong. He recommends contact between individuals rather than groups, especially when individuals of different groups share the same goal and communicate face-to-face. Paradoxically, the building of understanding, trust, and cooperation between groups is primarily an interpersonal challenge.

What are the implications of these findings for the pursuit of a human-centered society? It seems that most people can be attracted to Rousseau's worldview, at least locally if not globally. Such engagement is likely to be more successful in neighborhoods and communities initially, followed by linkages across neighborhoods and communities until the whole city or town is engaged.

This can be seeded in multiple places, particularly places where people routinely engage in interactions where cooperation is rewarded. Schools, churches, and social clubs are likely good targets. This bottom-up approach to fundamental change will be slow, but much more likely to succeed (Berman & Fox, 2023; Rouse, 2023), as elaborated in Chapter 8.

OVERVIEW OF BOOK

In the rest of this book, I employ the human-centered philosophy and paradigm to address the central tension of innovation versus exploitation. In Chapter 2, I explore the nature of innovation and exploitation in the context of the late-nineteenth and early twentieth centuries in the US, usually characterized as the Gilded Age when the "robber barons" accumulated enormous wealth until the Progressive Era tamed the exploitation.

Chapter 3 addresses the aerospace and defense ecosystem. The advances in these arenas have been enormous, both in terms of commercial transportation and arms races with our adversaries. Exploitation in this area concerns environmental impacts as well as the safety of aviation and other systems. On the defense side, the lack of a real marketplace invites waste, fraud, and abuse. The transparencies needed to mitigate such behaviors are often creatively thwarted.

Chapter 4 addresses computers and communications, while Chapter 5 considers the internet and social media. These highly interwoven ecosystems have transformed society over the past century or so. I discuss the central innovators, the nature of their innovations, and how exploitation emerged. We are in the midst of trying to thwart some aspects of this exploitation.

The next two chapters address traditional ecosystems. Chapter 6 considers health and wellness where the US spends much more per capita than any other OECD countries, yet achieve the worst health outcomes. Thus, exploitation is rampant as enormous profits accrue to would-be innovators, even when their offerings are not beneficial and certainly not innovations.

Chapter 7 focuses on energy and climate. There has been a steady stream of innovative ways to convert energy into useful work in transportation, production, and homes. Many of these innovations yield harmful environmental side effects, most notably pollution and global warming. This has led to substantial investments in renewable energy sources. Nevertheless, key stakeholders are continuing to strive to exploit their enormous investments in fossil fuels.

Chapter 8 addresses how all of these ecosystems, and society in general, can become much more human-centered. Society needs the many types of innovations that I discuss in this book. The possibility of exploitive advantages often drives would-be innovators to invest. Some of them succeed. A human-centered society inherently broadly shares the benefits of its innovations. This requires that we creatively constrain exploitation. As one executive suggested, we need to know how to pull feathers until just before the goose honks.

REFERENCES

Berman, G., & Fox, A. (2023). *Gradual: The Case for Incremental Change in a Radical Age.* Oxford: Oxford University Press.

Blinder, A.S. (2013). *After the Music Stopped: The Financial Crisis, the Response, and the Work Ahead.* New York: Penguin.

Boehm-Davis, D., Durso, F.T., & Lee, J.D. (2015). *APA Handbook of Human Systems Integration.* Washington, DC: American Psychological Association.

Booher, H.R. (Ed.). (1990). *Manprint: An Approach to Systems Integration.* New York: Reinhold.

Booher, H.R. (Ed.). (2003). *Handbook of Human Systems Integration.* New York: Wiley.

Bossidy, L., & Charan, R. (2009). *Execution: The Discipline of Getting Things Done.* Sydney: Currency.

DeLong, J.B. (2022). *Slouching Towards Utopia: An Economic History of the Twentieth Century*. New York: Basic Books.

Deming, W.E. (1982). *Out of Crisis*. Cambridge, MA: MIT Press.

Gordon, R.J. (2016). *The Rise and Fall of American Growth: The U.S. Standard of Living Since the Civil War*. Princeton, NJ: Princeton University Press.

Heller, N. (2017). Estonia, the digital republic. *The New Yorker*, December 11.

Hess, D.J. (2018). Social movements and energy democracy: Types and processes of mobilization. *Frontiers in Energy Research*, 6 (135). https://doi.org/10.3389/fenrg.2018.00135

Hoffman, B. (2003). Health care reform and social movements in the United States. *American Journal of Public Health*, 93 (1), 75–85.

Jarrett, C. (2018). The bad news on human nature in 10 findings from psychology. *Aeon*, December 5.

Keynes, J.M. (1936). *The General Theory of Employment, Interest and Money*. London: Palgrave Macmillan.

Khanna, R. (2022). *Dignity in a Digital Age: Making Tech Work for All of Us*. New York: Simon & Schuster.

Lewis, M. (2011). *The Big Short: Inside the Doomsday Machine*. New York: Norton.

Mokyr, J. (1992). *The Lever of Riches: Technological Creativity and Economic Progress*. Oxford: Oxford University Press.

NAP. (2021). *Human-AI Teaming: State of the Art and Research Needs*. Washington, DC: National Academies Press.

Norman, D.A. (2013). *Design of Everyday Things*. New York: Basic Books.

Norman, D.A. (2023). *Design for a Better World: Meaningful, Sustainable, Humanity Centered*. Cambridge, MA: MIT Press.

Polanyi, K. (1944). *The Great Transformation – The Political and Economic Origins of Our Time*. New York: Farrar & Rinehart.

Ramazzini, B. (1760). *Diseases of Workers*. New York: New York Academy of Sciences.

Rouse, W.B. (2010). *The Economics of Human Systems Integration: Valuation of Investments in Peoples Training and Education, Safety and Health, and Work Productivity*. Hoboken, NJ: Wiley.

Rouse, W.B. (1991). *Design or Success: A Human-Centered Approach to Designing Successful Products and Systems*. New York: Wiley.

Rouse, W.B. (1992). *Strategies for Innovation: Creating Successful Products, Systems, and Organizations*. New York: Wiley.

Rouse, W.B. (1993). *Catalysts for Change: Concepts and Principles for Enabling Innovation*. New York: Wiley.

Rouse, W.B. (2007). *People and Organizations: Explorations of Human-Centered Design*. New York: Wiley.

Rouse, W.B. (2014a). Human interaction with policy flight simulators. *Journal of Applied Ergonomics*, 45 (1), 72–77.

Rouse, W.B. (2014b). *A Century of Innovation: From Wooden Sailing Ships to Electric Railways, Computers, Space Travel and Internet*. Raleigh, NC: Lulu Press.

Rouse, W.B. (2015). *Modeling and Visualization of Complex Systems and Enterprises: Explorations of Physical, Human, Economic, and Social Phenomena*. Hoboken, NJ: John Wiley.

Rouse, W.B. (2019). *Computing Possible Futures: Model Based Explorations of "What if?"* Oxford: Oxford University Press.

Rouse, W.B. (2021). *Failure Management: Malfunctions of Technologies, Organizations and Society.* Oxford: Oxford University Press.

Rouse, W.B. (2022). *Transforming Public-Private Ecosystems: Understanding and Enabling Innovation in Complex Systems.* Oxford: Oxford University Press.

Rouse, W.B. (2023). *Beyond Quick Fixes: Addressing the Complexity & Uncertainties of Contemporary Society.* Oxford: Oxford University Press.

Rouse, W.B., & Spohrer, J.C. (2018). Automating versus augmenting intelligence. *Journal of Enterprise Transformation*, https://doi.org/10.1080/19488289.2018.1424059

Salvendy, G., & Karwowski, W. (2021). *Handbook of Human Factors and Ergonomics* (5th Edition). New York: Wiley.

Sheridan, T.B. (1985). Forty-five years of man-machine systems. *Proceedings of IFAC Conference on Man-Machine Systems*, Varese, Italy.

Sheridan, T.B. (1992). *Telerobotics, Automation, and Human Supervisory Control.* Cambridge, MA: MIT Press.

Sheridan, T.B. (2022). *Telepresence: Actual and Virtual: Promises and Perils of Converging New Realities.* Boca Raton, FL: CRC Press.

Sheridan, T.B., & Ferrell, W.R. (1974). *Man-Machine Systems: Information, Control, and Decision Models of Human Performance.* Cambridge, MA: MIT Press.

Shneiderman, B. (2022). *Human-Centered AI.* Oxford: Oxford University Press.

Van Heertum, R., & Torres, C.A. (2011). Educational reform in the U.S. in the past 30 years: Great expectations and the fading American dream. In L. Olmos, R. Van Heertum & C.A. Torres, Eds., *Educating The Global Citizen.* Sharjah: Bentham Science.

Van Lange, P. (2019). People are naturally good, but groups are not (really). *Psychology Today*, December 24.

Wapshott, N. (2011). *Keynes Hayek: The Clash that Defined Modern Economics.* New York: Norton.

Ward, A.F. (2012). Scientists probe human nature – And discover we are good after all. *Scientific American*, November 20.

Wrangham, R. (2019). *The Goodness Paradox.* New York: Pantheon Books.

Wundt, W. (1904). *Principles of Physiological Psychology.* New York: Macmillan.

2

Innovators and Exploiters

INTRODUCTION

My overall thesis is that innovation and economic growth are key enablers of a human-centered society. A continually rising tide can lift all boats, although this has not always been the case. A key driver of innovation, in terms of translating inventions to market value propositions, is entrepreneurs' expectations of being able to exploit market opportunities for substantial economic gains. However, people are unlikely to accept exploitation perpetually.

I will address innovation first, then exploitation. As briefly noted in Chapter 1, economists are often concerned about sources of innovation and economic growth. I find Mokyr's (1992, 2017) arguments and illustrations particularly compelling. He asserts that technology has long been the driver. Market innovations, often technology-driven, have long led to new markets, new jobs, and enabled consumers.

I noted earlier that there seems to be an emerging consensus that the US leadership in innovation has waned. Gordon (2016) has argued that 1870–1970 was the United States' century of innovation. I made the same argument, based on the same line of reasoning (Rouse, 2014). The rationale for 1970 as the end point is that social networking is not as compelling as electricity and indoor plumbing.

More recently, DeLong (2022) proposed 1870–2007 as the country's "long century" of innovation, ending with the onset of the Great Recession. This just extends the argument but does not change it. It does, however, end the innovation window before the onslaught of social media, which certainly has been a compelling source of disruption. I return to this topic in considerable detail in Chapter 5.

DOI: 10.4324/9781003462361-2

INNOVATION

I begin consideration of the nature of innovation by reviewing some classic findings. I then discuss differences among domains. The notion of "hype cycles" is used to illustrate the dynamics of market penetration. I then summarize a few classic observations.

Background

Everett Rogers (1962) wrote the classic *Diffusion of Innovations*. He differentiates five stages of diffusion:

- Innovators (2.5%)
- Early adopters (13.5%)
- Early majority (34%)
- Late majority (34%)
- Laggards (16%)

It is difficult to sustain investments if customers are limited to innovators and early adopters. Penetrating the early majority is often a huge challenge for would-be innovators.

Geoffrey Moore (1991) in *Crossing the Chasm* shows

> there is a vast chasm between the early adopters and the early majority. While early adopters are willing to sacrifice for the advantage of being first, the early majority waits until they know that the technology actually offers improvements in productivity. The challenge for innovators and marketers is to narrow this chasm and ultimately accelerate adoption across every segment.

In *Transforming Public-Private Ecosystems* (Rouse, 2022), I review my experiences in addressing and trying to advance innovation. Invention is the creation of a new process or device, while innovation is the creation of change in the marketplace (Rouse, 1992, 1993).

The marketplace can be for art, automobiles, computers, consumer products, or medicine, to name just a few ecosystems. From this broader perspective, innovation is context-dependent. Some innovations are driven by inventions. Others are driven by needs – necessity is the mother of invention. New understanding drives others, e.g., the discovery of bacteria.

In the context of public-private ecosystems, markets can be conceptualized as constituencies. Constituencies can be military missions, public health, or perhaps a targeted group, for example, patients or students. An intended innovation becomes an actual innovation once the targeted constituencies embrace it.

Differences Among Domains

Consider the differences between automobiles and medicine. The underlying phenomena are quite different. Automotive is driven by inventions in terms of originations of technologies, manufacturing processes, and value propositions. Medicine is driven by epidemics, war, and biomedical research. Both of these timelines are well documented.

Measures of innovation depend on the context. The percentage of sales from new offerings makes sense for automobiles, but not healthcare delivery. The number of deaths avoided is likely a better metric for medicine. Increased Quality Adjusted Life Years is another metric. Notice the contrast. For automobiles, the key metrics are about what *did* happen – sales – while for medicine, the key metrics are about what *did not* happen – poor quality of life and deaths.

Innovations in consumer or business markets have been subjects of much research, but there can be innovations in, for example, scientific techniques. Of course, one could argue that the scientific community is then the constituency. Thus, innovation can be said to happen when a targeted population changes how it does things.

In automobiles, we look at what people buy. In science, we look at what people cite. For consumers, we might look at what people consume or buy. In medicine, it may be clinicians voting, not patients. Same for expert service providers in general. Thus, the population of potential adopters targeted is key.

Another factor is the infrastructure needed to adopt something so it can become an innovation. This held up electricity but, once powerplants and utility lines were in place, eased the adoption of television – and many other inventions. A key to innovation, assuming needed infrastructure, is adoption by some populations.

Hype Cycles

Gartner (2020) has popularized the notion of hype cycles to include several phases:

- A potential technology breakthrough kicks things off.
- Early publicity produces a number of success stories.
- Interest wanes as experiments and implementations fail to deliver.
- More instances of the benefits of the technology start to crystallize and become understood.
- Mainstream adoption starts to take off, as criteria for adoption are more clearly defined.

The exuberance of marketing is relatively recent. I could not find any *New York Times* articles portending the likely advent of indoor plumbing and electricity. It is interesting to imagine hype cycles for these important innovations. It took well over 50 years for Edison's vision to affect almost every home. It took over a century for the majority of homes in the developed world to have indoor plumbing. In contrast, the smart phone became ubiquitous in ten years.

How could the innovation of the smart phone happen so much more quickly? The answer, as noted earlier, is infrastructure. The smart phone could leverage the Internet and cellular technologies, not to mention electricity. Such infrastructure was not available to Edison, nor was it to Isaiah Rogers who first demonstrated indoor plumbing in 1829 in the Tremont Hotel in Boston.

The relevant metric here is quite straightforward. What percentage of the population is benefitting from the innovation? When every Accord or Camry comes with a backup camera as standard equipment, the camera technology has made it. When every vehicle has this capability, few could imagine a vehicle without it. Backup cameras, at this point, no longer seem like innovations.

Summary

The phenomenon of innovation seems broadly applicable, but the context matters in terms of the nature of what is considered innovative and how it is measured. New products, services, ideas, experiences, etc. have to be assessed and measured differently. Such considerations concern monitoring and projecting potential innovations.

Another essential concern is how best to foster innovation. In all domains, the vast majority of inventions do not lead to innovations. Most people and organizations are much more inventive than innovative, despite the claims on resumes and marketing brochures. Innovation is hard work.

Edison famously said, "Genius is one percent inspiration and ninety-nine percent perspiration." The perspiration is central to transforming a creative invention into a true innovation. The enthusiasms of many people and organizations wane when they come to realize this, whether they are artists, clinicians, engineers, or politicians.

The distinction between invention and innovation has important implications. Many folks create new processes or devices, but very few of these creations make it to the market. I have worked with over 100 companies and agencies. Many of them consider their organizations to be innovative. After my review of their technology investment portfolios, I often told them that were very inventive, but not so innovative. The changes in the marketplace that they had created were not what would be expected from innovators.

Yet there is another phenomenon that I have encountered working with hundreds of organizations. Many inventors simply do not believe that the inherently low probabilities of success apply to them. Consequently, they doggedly invest themselves, almost irrationally, in getting their creation to "market," whatever that means in their domain. While the odds remain very low, we all benefit from this determination and the few that actually become innovations.

EXPLOITATION

Exploitation involves seeking unfair advantage in a marketplace or among a constituency to accrue inordinate financial gains at the expense of others, often while also exposing them to environmental, health, and safety risks. Exploitation has a rich history, with the powerful controlling the weak, often as slaves who lived miserable lives.

Tragedy of the Commons

New England was heavily forested when the colonists arrived in the seventeenth century. It is heavily forested today, particularly in northern states. However, the forests one sees today are "new growth." The earlier forests were denuded to support the region's wood economy. Annie Proulx's novel *Barkskins* (2016) chronicles this era.

The colonists used wood for everything. They cut down trees to build homes, roads, bridges, and ships. Shipbuilding in New England was a major industry. My great-great-grandfather founded a shipyard and later was superintendent of construction for a steamship line, originally with wooden ships but later iron and then steel.

Ships were also built for fishing and hunting whales. This affected what goods people in New England could trade. There was much trade between New England and other regions or countries such as England. New England would export resources like fish and lumber. In return, unfortunately, New England would receive slaves that were sold to plantations in the south.

New England and the rest of the country moved from a wood economy to a fossil fuel economy – coal, oil, and gas-fueled industries. Private automobiles emerged in the early twentieth century, enabling by mid-century vast suburbs and increasing traffic and congestion. This has resulted in vast amounts of carbon dioxide (CO_2) emitted into the atmosphere.

The wood economy is an example of a tragedy of the commons, classically characterized by Garrett Hardin (1968). Much more recently Elinor Ostrom has articulated principles for governing the commons. I discuss these principles in Chapter 8. We need mechanisms to mitigate human tendencies to exploit common resources.

Examples of Exploitation

Brook (2013) provides an interesting set of stories in *A History of Future Cities*, including discussions of 200 years of exploitation:

- 1661   Bombay, established in third century BCE, becomes a British settlement
- 1703   St. Petersburg founded
- 1843   Shanghai, established in 1291, becomes a British settlement

These cities were gleaming places of modernity. Surrounding these cities were large classes of people stuck in unhealthy, uneducated poverty. Nevertheless, they could see what modernity was like and they eventually revolted, not just at the ballot box, but also by physically attacking the privileged. This has happened many times before. If the needs of the poor and downtrodden are substantially ignored, they eventually revolt.

Gandhi (2021) reports on the transcontinental railroad's dark costs of exploited labor and stolen lands. The railroad was built during 1863–1869 with 20,000 Chinese workers. Chinese laborers earned between half and two-thirds of what Euro-American laborers did and had to pay for their food. In the summer of 1867, thousands of Chinese workers organized the largest labor stoppage in America up to that date to demand both equal pay and better working conditions. Railroad bosses ultimately broke the strike by withholding food rations and threatening violence, and the workers' demands were denied.

Von Drehle (2006) chronicles the history of the Triangle Shirtwaist Fire in 1911. This fire killed 146 people – in a locked eighth floor of a garment factory in Greenwich Village. Almost all of them were immigrant women and children. This led to the transformation of the labor code of New York State and to the adoption of fire safety measures that served as a model for the whole country. The fire helped unite organized labor and reform-minded politicians like progressive New York Governor Alfred E. Smith and Senator Robert F. Wagner.

Boissoneault (2017) describes the coal mining massacre America forgot. West Virginia was and is coal country. The industry's massive corporations built homes, general stores, schools, and churches near the mines. For the miners, company houses were abysmal, wages were low, and state politicians supported wealthy coal company owners rather than miners. The system was more like feudalism than democracy. Violence was inevitable and emerged in 1920. Martial law was declared and federal troops had to intervene.

It might seem that things are much better now, but exploitation is alive and well. Scheiber (2023) reports that many companies provide salaries just above the federal cutoff of $35,500 to frontline workers and mislabel them as managers to deny them overtime. People work 60 to 80 hours per week but get paid for 40. Employers are trying to increase profits by understaffing and overworking existing staff. This is just on the edge of illegal.

Harnett (2023) describes how health inequity maps out across America. Evangeline Parish (LA), Bronx County (NY), and Navajo County (AZ) rank within the 99th percentile for social vulnerability – determined using 14 census metrics related to income and access to food, water, and transportation – and are designated medically underserved by the federal government. Thus, inequity is not specific to geography, culture, or politics. Exploitation is unfortunately diverse, equitable, and inclusive.

O'Donovan (2023) describes how Amazon's belt-tightening is affecting towns across the US. Communities across the country have lined up to offer incentives to attract jobs, which can be a boon, particularly in areas where traditional industries have dried up or moved abroad. Small towns around the country that were counting on an Amazon boost are nonetheless disappointed when those projects do not come to fruition. They have been exploited in the sense of having been lured into having expectations that their local economies can recover.

Innovators hope to achieve a "break out" and achieve sufficient market share to have some level of control over revenues and profits. This tends to require exploiting sources of costs – employees, benefits, safety – to provide offerings at competitive prices. Once they are successful, these practices are too well ingrained to be reversed. External forces, described later in this chapter are needed, to mitigate exploitation.

ROBBER BARONS

Let's consider five US luminaries who in the nineteenth and early twentieth centuries epitomized innovators whose success enabled them to become exploiters (Morris, 2005). They directly and indirectly exploited competitors and consumers by creating monopolies that could control markets, particularly pricing. They ruthlessly cut costs, in part by exploiting workers.

Of course, seeking monopoly positions to enable enormous profits was – and still is – a common business objective. Stock market investors reward companies that do this. This involves having the highest prices customers will accept and the lowest costs employees can endure. As I noted in the brief history of exploitation, the powerful exploiting the weak to maximize wealth is a well-honored tradition.

Cornelius Vanderbilt (1794–1877) built his wealth in railroads and shipping. By the early 1840s, Vanderbilt's apparent intentions were to take control of all steamer and rail lines between New York and Boston. He managed to gain complete control of two of the four lines and dominant positions in the other two. However, in 1847 he started extricating himself from these investments, probably because he realized that competition was rapidly growing. The New York and New Haven Railroad, over which he had no control, was about to be opened. He was also aware of the emerging formation of the Fall River Line – initially called the Bay State Steamboat Company.

Starting in 1863, Cornelius Vanderbilt shifted his attention from steamboats to consolidating railroads (Stiles, 2009). On May 18, 1863, he was elected president of the New York and Harlem Railroad. On December 11, 1867, Vanderbilt became president of the New York Central Railroad. The investment in the New York Central alone equaled one-quarter of the investment in all of manufacturing in the US.

John D. Rockefeller (1839–1937) founded Standard Oil in 1870. It became the Standard Oil Trust in 1881. Rockefeller's wealth soared as kerosene and gasoline grew in importance, and he became the richest person in the country, controlling 90% of all oil in the United States at his peak. He was well known for cutting prices below costs to force competitors out of business.

Standard Oil was broken up in 1911 as a result of a lawsuit brought against it by the US government in 1906 under the Sherman Antitrust Act of 1890. Standard Oil of New Jersey, the entity controlling Standard Oil at the time of the breakup, has since continued as ExxonMobil, the largest investor-owned oil company in the world. Many other companies are direct descendants of Standard Oil (e.g., Chevron) or were acquired (e.g., by BP).

Andrew Carnegie (1835–1919) built Pittsburgh's Carnegie Steel Company, which he sold to J.P. Morgan in 1901 for almost $10 billion (today). This formed the basis of the US Steel Corporation. After selling Carnegie Steel, he surpassed John D. Rockefeller as the richest American for the next several years. An attempt to break up US Steel in 1920 failed when the Supreme Court voted 4–3 that US Steel did not violate the Sherman Antitrust Act of 1890.

Carnegie libraries are those built with money donated by philanthropist Andrew Carnegie. A total of 2,509 Carnegie libraries were built between 1883 and 1929, including some belonging to public and university library systems. The Carnegie Library of Washington DC is now known as the Apple Carnegie Library, due to the company's substantial investment in its renovation. The original library was dedicated on January 7, 1903. It was Washington DC's first desegregated public building.

John P. Morgan (1837–1913) was an American financier and investment banker who dominated corporate finance on Wall Street throughout the Gilded Age. As the head of the banking firm that ultimately became known as J.P. Morgan and Co., he was the driving force behind the wave of industrial consolidation in the United States spanning the late nineteenth and early twentieth centuries (Chernow, 1990).

Morgan brokered the formation of US Steel by merging Andrew Carnegie's Carnegie Steel Company, Elbert Gary's Federal Steel Company, and William Moore's National Steel Company. Morgan also led the merger of Edison Electric with Thomson-Houston in 1892 to form General Electric and resolve patent disputes. Thomson-Houston's chief executive Charles A. Coffin took over the poorly managed Edison Electric. Morgan acted as the ad hoc central banker of the US, averting economic disasters of 1895 and 1907.

Henry Ford (1861–1947) was chief engineer for the Edison Electric Illuminating Company in Detroit in 1893 at age 30. In 1896, Ford built his first car in a shed behind his house (Ingrassia, 2012). From 1901 to 1908, 501 automobile companies were founded in the US – 60% folded within a couple of years. He chafed under the conflict between being an inventor and needing a large, well-capitalized organization to bring his inventions to market.

He founded the Ford Motor Company in 1903. By the spring of 1905, they were producing 25 Model As per day and employing 300 workers. The Model T was announced in the autumn of 1908 and by 1920 accounted for almost half the vehicles in the US (Watts, 2006). It was the first car with fully interchangeable parts.

Ford emerged as more a folk hero rather than an outright robber baron like Rockefeller, Vanderbilt, or Morgan. In early 1914, Ford announced a starting wage of $5 per day, roughly double what it had been, while also reducing the workday from nine to eight hours. His goal was to enable his workers to buy his cars.

He was the chief developer of the assembly line technique of mass production. Ford created the first automobile that middle-class Americans could afford, and his conversion of the automobile from an expensive luxury into an accessible conveyance profoundly impacted the landscape of the twentieth century.

Philanthropy

The robber barons became philanthropists later in life. Vanderbilt founded Vanderbilt University (1873) with a $1 million endowment ($25 million today), which has grown, from many sources, to $11 billion. By the third generation, the family had squandered much of the wealth on, for example, palatial homes in Newport, Rhode Island, and vast estates in Asheville, North Carolina, (Stiles, 2009; Kiernan, 2017).

The Rockefeller Foundation was founded in 1913; current assets total $6.3 billion. The Carnegie Foundation began in 1905; its current assets are $3.6 billion. The Ford Foundation was founded in 1936; current assets equal $12.5 billion. The Sloan Foundation was founded in 1934; its current assets are $2 billion. I include Alfred P. Sloan of GM in this compilation as he was Henry Ford's nemesis.

J.P. Morgan donated millions to charities and public institutions. He gave art collections to the Metropolitan Museum of Art, the American Museum of Natural History, the American Academy in Rome, Wadsworth Atheneum, and Yale University. His charity continues through the JP Morgan Chase Foundation, with assets of $300 million.

Carnegie formalized the importance of philanthropy with his Gospel of Wealth. He argued that extremely wealthy Americans should actively engage in philanthropy and charity in order to close the widening gap between rich and poor. One of his most famous quotes is "The man who dies rich thus dies disgraced" (Carnegie, 1889).

Thus, these five innovators and exploiters tended to generously give back to society. We will see that this behavior continues with current innovators in later chapters. Nevertheless, the desire to control markets, create monopolies, and maximize profits remains a dominant force in markets and societies.

THE GILDED AGE

The Gilded Age was a period of rapid industrialization in America from 1865 to 1898. It was characterized by the extreme concentration of wealth in a few individuals, such as those noted above. Many others lived in poverty. Political corruption and exploitation of immigrant labor are often associated with this era.

Corruption and graft permeated every level of American politics. Campaigns promised patronage and civil service positions in order to win elections and access to infrastructure that benefitted corporations over small-scale businesses. This corruption met various forms of resistance, which were often suppressed.

The expansion of industry and transportation and the lack of an income tax gave rise to a new wealthy class of people. Among the best known of the entrepreneurs who became known, pejoratively, as robber barons during the Gilded Age were Cornelius Vanderbilt, John D. Rockefeller, Andrew Carnegie, and J.P. Morgan. Henry Ford was an outlier, greatly due to his $5 daily wages.

Newport, Rhode Island, played a big role during this period, between roughly 1870 and 1910, as some of the world's wealthiest people came to the "City-by-the-Sea" to build summertime "cottages" along the waterfront. The Breakers, perhaps the most famous cottage, included 70 rooms. Cornelius Vanderbilt II, grandson of the innovator, built this cottage.

Many of the cottage owners lived in New York City. The society section of The *New York Times* had a Newport section each week indicating which of the owners would be in Newport for the coming weekend. They could travel from New York to Newport on the elegant Fall River Line, which was owned by a J.P. Morgan company. My great-great-grandfather, George P. Peirce, was in charge of ship design for the Fall River Line. A visit by his son Charles to George's home in Newport was reported in the *Times* Newport section.

There are varying opinions on when the Gilded Age ended. A common opinion is that it ended with The Panic of 1893. The stock market plummeted as businesses that had borrowed heavily to invest in railroads went bankrupt. The value of crops in the American South and West fell. Unemployment rose as high as 19%. The crash threw the power of the wealthy – and the powerlessness of labor – into stark relief.

This period also prompted the "muckrakers" to uncover corruption. Ida Tarbell's *The History of the Standard Oil Company*, a 19-part series published in the magazine *McClures* in the early 1900s, and Upton Sinclair's *The Jungle* (Sinclair, 1906), which focused on the meatpacking industry, are renowned instances of exposing corruption.

There was increased populism due to resentment of the concentration of wealth amidst widespread poverty. I grew up in Portsmouth, Rhode Island, on the other end of Aquidneck Island from Newport. A significant portion of the island's population provided services, food, coal, etc. to the wealthy in Newport. Resentment of the lifestyles of the wealthy was a common and popular topic.

These forces fueled the Progressive Era and a variety of reforms, which I discuss in the next section. It was a period of widespread social activism and political reform across the United States focused on defeating corruption, monopoly, waste, and inefficiency. The presidency of Theodore Roosevelt served as a major catalyst for change.

THE PROGRESSIVE ERA

There is rough agreement that this era began around 1896 and ended in 1917 as the US joined the Allies in World War I. Progressives addressed problems caused by rapid industrialization, urbanization, immigration, and political corruption, as well as the enormous concentration of wealth in monopolies. In particular, progressives were concerned with the spread of slums, poverty, and what they perceived as the exploitation of labor.

Rather than a single integrated movement, there were multiple overlapping movements, fighting perceived social, political, and economic ills. The intentions of these movements included advancing democracy, scientific methods, regulating businesses, protecting the natural environment, and improving working conditions in factories and living conditions of the urban poor.

Significant legislation and regulation included the Sherman Antitrust Act of 1890. This federal statute prohibits activities that restrict interstate commerce and competition in the marketplace. It outlaws any contract, conspiracy, or combination of business interests in restraint of foreign or interstate trade. The Clayton Antitrust Act of 1914 expanded these antitrust regulations.

As mentioned earlier, Standard Oil was broken up in 1911 as a result of a lawsuit brought against it by the US government in 1906 under the Sherman Antitrust Act of 1890. Note that it took five years to reach a ruling. A similar attempt to break up US Steel in 1920 failed when the

Supreme Court voted that US Steel did not violate the Sherman and Clayton Antitrust Acts.

Several states passed legislation helpful to labor, such as laws establishing a minimum wage for women, maximum work hours, workmen's compensation, and abolishing child labor. However, it was not until 1935 that the National Labor Relations Act, also known as the Wagner Act, guaranteed the right of private sector employees to organize into trade unions, engage in collective bargaining, and take collective action such as strikes.

Progressive Era legislation countered those who had cornered whole segments of America's economy using predatory pricing, exclusive dealings, and anti-competitive mergers to drive local businesses to ruin. Teddy Roosevelt (1858–1919) was a central figure in the progressive movement throughout his presidency (1901–1909) and beyond.

He vigorously promoted the conservation movement, emphasizing the efficient use of natural resources. He dramatically expanded the system of national parks and national forests. After 1906, he moved to the left, denouncing the rich, attacking trusts, proposing a welfare state, and supporting labor unions (Goodwin, 2013).

Other important progressive legislation included the Federal Reserve Act of 1913. The Federal Reserve System was created to address banking panics and to foster a sound banking system. The motivating force for this included banking panics that occurred in 1873, 1893, and 1907 with incipient panics in 1884 and 1890. After the Federal Reserve Act was passed in 1913, there were several full-scale banking panics in 1930, 1931, 1932, and 1933, all associated with the consequences of the Great Depression.

As noted earlier, the Progressive Era ended with the US entry into WWI in late 1917. In the 1920s, the Progressive movement began to be supplanted by several different movements, e.g., women's suffrage. Progressive victories caused activists to lose momentum. The progressive wing of the Republican Party was weakened by the party splits of 1912 and 1924, engendered by Theodore Roosevelt. The progressive wing of the Democratic Party was subsumed under the broader New Deal coalition of Franklin Roosevelt. Foreign policy matters were increasingly focused on the buildup to World War II. Progressive issues faded compared to the interventionist/isolationist split.

A PATTERN

Figure 2.1 depicts a typical pattern of innovation and exploitation, as evidenced by the chronicles of the robber barons. I illustrate how this pattern plays out in other domains in later chapters. In Chapter 8, I explore how this pattern can be anticipated and managed to foster a human-centered society.

Consider how the ten elements of this pattern typically play out. It seems reasonable to argue that the first four elements follow Mokyr's model of technology development and economic growth.

- Technologies emerge and mature
- Entrepreneurs invest in development
- Competitors launch offerings
- Competitors gain market shares

FIGURE 2.1
Typical pattern of innovation and exploitation

The next three elements depend on the economic, political, and social context of innovation and exploitation. For example, the contexts of the US and Scandinavia are quite different in terms of degrees of freedom allowed.

- Monopolistic practices emerge
- Profits grow as competitors withdraw
- Enormous wealth accrues to shareholders

The last three elements also differ by context. If the above three elements are inherently inhibited, the final three may involve more tuning than transformation. In the US, these final three may take many years, perhaps decades, to happen.

- Monopolistic practices questioned by media
- Public pressure for reform emerges
- Legislators and regulators curb practices

In later chapters, I consider how the pattern in Figure 2.1 differs across domains, particularly relative to what is being exploited, e.g., money vs. safety vs. environment.

CONCLUSIONS

The sociopolitical ecosystem eventually reacts to the tension between innovation and exploitation. New technologies displace old technologies and the jobs associated with older practices. Workers push back against such changes, but superior technologies ultimately prevail. Workers, and society in general, eventually benefit from these changes.

Innovations can lead to exploitation. Several common phenomena emerge. Monopolies find that they do not need to invest to compete. When profits are constrained, they pad costs to increase revenues. Poor construction practices (e.g., design, materials, labor) are employed to increase profits. Safety consequences are ignored and avoided.

Profits are motivated by greed, but also by the scorecards entrepreneurs tend to keep. Winning can become as important as wealth. However, conspicuous practices of concentrated wealth are eventually noticed and uncovered by the public. This results in public pressure for reform and, sooner or later, political initiatives to curb exploitation.

As I illustrate in later chapters, this pattern repeats itself in many ecosystems. Knowing that this is going to happen, we can anticipate and manage it better. It should not be a surprise when innovations precipitate exploitation. Key stakeholders should be prepared to address this fundamental tension and creatively resolve it. The goal is to sustain innovation instincts, but transition from exploitation to broad benefits for society. The overall goal is a creative balance.

REFERENCES

Boissoneault, L. (2017). The coal mining massacre America forgot. *Smithsonian Magazine*, April 25.

Brook, D. (2013). *A History of Future Cities*. New York: Norton.

Carnegie, A. (1889). *The Gospel of Wealth and Other Timely Essays*. New York: The Century Company.

Chernow, R. (1990). *The House of Morgan: An American Banking Dynasty and the Rise of Modern Finance*. New York: Grove Press.

DeLong, J.B. (2022). *Slouching Towards Utopia: An Economic History of the Twentieth Century*. New York: Basic Books.

Gandhi, L. (2021). The transcontinental railroad's dark costs: Exploited labor, stolen lands. www.history.com, October 8.

Gartner. (2020). *Gartner Hype Cycle*. https://www.gartner.com/en/research/methodologies/gartner-hype-cycle. Accessed 08/07/20.

Goodwin, D.K. (2013). *The Bully Pulpit: Theodore Roosevelt, William Howard Taft, and the Golden Age of Journalism*. New York: Simon & Schuster.

Gordon, R.J. (2016). *The Rise and Fall of American Growth: The U.S. Standard of Living Since the Civil War*. Princeton, NJ: Princeton University Press.

Harden, G. (1986). The tragedy of the commons. *Science*, 162 (3859), 1243–1248.

Harnett, K. (2023). How health inequity maps out across America. *Modern Healthcare*, March 5.

Ingrassia, P. (2012). *Engines of Change: A History of the American Dream in Fifteen Cars*. New York: Simon & Schuster.

Isaacson, W. (2014). *The Innovators: How a Group of Hackers, Geniuses, and Geeks Created the Digital Revolution*. New York: Simon & Schuster.

Kiernan, D. (2017). *The Last Castle: The Epic Story of Love, Loss, and American Royalty in the Nation's Largest Home*. New York: Atria Books.

Mokyr, J. (1992). *The Lever of Riches: Technological Creativity and Economic Progress*. Oxford: Oxford University Press.

Mokyr, J. (2017). *A Culture of Growth: The Origins of the Modern Economy*. Princeton, NJ: Princeton University Press.

Moore, G.A. (1991). *Crossing the Chasm: Marketing and Selling Technology Projects to Mainstream Customers.* New York: Harper.

Morris, C. (2005). *The Tycoons: How Andrew Carnegie, John D. Rockefeller, Jay Gould, and J.P. Morgan Invented the American Supereconomy.* New York: Henry Holt.

O'Donovan, C. (2023). Amazon's belt tightening affects towns across the US. *New York Times,* March 7.

Ostrom, E. (2015). *Governing the Commons: The Evolution of Institutions for Collective Action.* Cambridge: Cambridge University Press.

Proulx, A. (2016). *Barkskins: A Novel.* New York: Schribners.

Rogers, E. (1962). *Diffusion of Innovations* (5th Edition is 2003). New York: Simon and Schuster.

Rouse, W.B. (1992). *Strategies for Innovation: Creating Successful Products, Systems, and Organizations.* New York: Wiley.

Rouse, W.B. (1993). *Catalysts for Change: Concepts and Principles for Enabling Innovation.* New York: Wiley.

Rouse, W.B. (2014). *A Century of Innovation: From Wooden Sailing Ships to Electric Railways, Computers, Space Travel and Internet.* Raleigh, NC: Lulu Press.

Rouse, W.B. (2022). *Transforming Public-Private Ecosystems: Understanding and Enabling Innovation in Complex Systems.* Oxford: Oxford University Press.

Rouse, W.B. (2023). *Bigger Pictures for Innovation: Creating Solutions, Managing Enterprises & Influencing Policies.* Oxfordshire: Routledge.

Scheiber, N. (2023). You're now a manager, forget about overtime pay. *New York Times,* March 6.

Sinclair, U. (1906). *The Jungle.* New York: Doubleday.

Stiles, T.J. (2009). *The First Tycoon: The Epic Life of Cornelius Vanderbilt.* New York: Knopf.

von Drehle, D. (2006). Uncovering the history of the Triangle Shirtwaist Fire. *Smithsonian Magazine,* August.

Watts, S. (2006). *The People's Tycoon: Henry Ford and the American Century.* New York: Vintage Books.

3

Transportation and Defense

The vignettes in Chapter 2 addressed shipping, railroads, energy, steel, and finance. In this chapter I look at transportation in more detail, adding automobiles and airplanes, with a brief foray into defense, a reasonable segue from airplanes. I first discuss innovations in transportation and then consider the resulting societal exploitations. I then elaborate on the nature of these exploitations in the defense industry.

INNOVATIONS IN TRANSPORTATION

The history of the transportation industry is, in many ways, synonymous with the history of the growth and industrialization of the US. Before the early 1800s, the dominant forms of transportation – horse, stagecoach, sailing ship, and so on – had not changed substantially in centuries. Then, within roughly 100 years, we had steamboats, railroads, automobiles, and aircraft. In the process of moving from stagecoaches and canal boats to jet planes, humankind changed the speed at which it traveled by a factor of 100. Trips that once took days, now take minutes.

These substantial changes in technology resulted in the formation of many thousands of companies. Most of these companies failed. Some prospered briefly. Very few prospered for a long period. Only a handful are still with us today. In this chapter, as well as the next several chapters, I explore the nature of this phenomenon.

As outlined in *Start Where You Are* (Rouse, 1996), I discuss these historical innovators as their enterprises transitioned through several common market situations summarized in Table 3.1.

DOI: 10.4324/9781003462361-3

TABLE 3.1

Ten Common Business Situations

Situation	Definition
Vision Quest	A situation where you are trying to create a relationship with the marketplace, usually for products and services that are ahead of the market's expressed needs and wants.
Evolution	A situation where the development of your relationship with the marketplace takes substantial time as your technologies, processes, and overall market proposition mature.
Crossover	A situation where either your success depends on importing key technologies and processes from other domains, or your success depends on exporting your technologies or processes to other markets.
Crossing the Chasm	A situation where you must transition from selling to innovators and early adopters to a more pragmatic relationship with the early majority in the broader marketplace; originated by Geoffrey Moore in his book *Crossing the Chasm* (1991).
Steady Growth	A situation where sales and profits repeatedly increase as your relationship with the market becomes strongly established; quite often, market share increases in an overall market that is also increasing.
Consolidation	A situation where the number of competitors and the fierceness of the competition increase to the point that price cutting and increased costs result in many mergers, acquisitions, and business failures.
Silent War	A situation where you do not recognize competing companies or technologies, or perhaps recognize and discount them; they thereby become strong competitors while you offer little if any resistance; originated by Ira Magaziner and Mark Patinkin in their book *The Silent War* (1989).
Paradigm Lost	A situation where your technologies, processes, market propositions, etc. become obsolete, often suddenly, due to new approaches and competitors, which results in damage to your relationship with the marketplace; phrase originated by John Casti in his book *Paradigms Lost* (1989).
Commodity Trap	A situation where most or all competitors are selling the same products or services due to de facto or actual standards, with the result that you must focus on quality, service, and price as the dominant competitive attributes.
Process	A situation where improvements of processes, rather than new product innovations, are the central competitive issue; substantial investments are usually required if you are to beat your competitors' quality, service, and prices.

These innovators transitioned among these market situations as shown in Figure 3.1. Thus, underlying the success of translating inventions into innovations is a dynamic set of relationships involving all the competitors at particular points in time. A few prosper. Most fail. We are better off because of this.

Steamboats

Robert Fulton is traditionally credited with the invention of the steamboat in 1807. He was fortunate, however, to be able to build on a variety of earlier

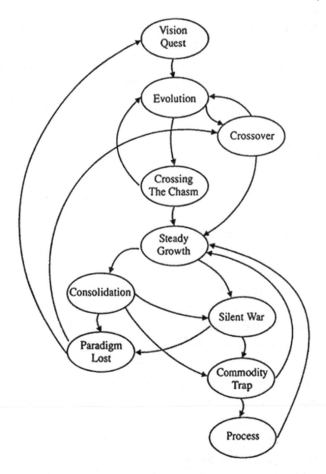

FIGURE 3.1
Typical transitions among common business situations

efforts. The French had experimented with steam-powered boats almost 200 years prior to Fulton's success. Several steamboats were demonstrated following James Watt's improvements to the steam engine in 1775. Fulton had also developed a steamboat in France a few years before his unveiling of the Clermont in the US.

The long gestation period for steamboat technology is typical. If viewed from a broad perspective, these stories reflect evolution, not revolution. Technology slowly matures until someone – usually not the originator, who typically is long gone – is able to transform technological invention into market innovation. Then, growth often occurs quite quickly.

With Fulton's demonstration in 1807, the steamboat industry blossomed. By 1819, a steamboat had sailed from Savannah, Georgia, to Russia. The first all-steam crossing, without the use of supporting sails, occurred in 1827. By the mid-1800s, transatlantic steamboat lines were competing. For example, the American Collins Line, formed to compete with the British Cunard Line, temporarily dominated Atlantic trade with their paddle wheelers that could achieve 13 knots.

The technological push for ever-increasing speeds was a key element of the competition. A particularly important contribution in this regard was the steam turbine, which was patented by Charles Parsons in 1884. Safety was also a critical element of the competition. While the first iron-hulled boat was demonstrated in Scotland in 1787, it was not until 1850 that iron hulls became predominant. After 1880, steel hulls were dominant. Evolution continued.

As with most emerging industries, the steamboat industry experienced both steady growth and consolidation situations, complicated by the fact that the railroads were struggling for maturity at the same time. Dunbaugh (1992) notes that the many steamer lines never seemed able to keep up with increasing demand and advances in technology. There was a constant push to outdo each other in terms of speed, safety, and various amenities. I can imagine those involved with this industry having many late-night discussions analogous to those in the computer and communications industries in Chapter 4 about, for example, chips, computers, networks, and, most recently, digital devices.

Thus, we see what was, at the time, a "high-tech" industry racing, relative to the time scale in their era, to accelerate new technologies into use. We also see increasing numbers of players, including railroads, competing for market share. The result was consolidation as companies gave up, or were forced to give up, due to skimpy if any profits.

In contrast to later examples, it appears that the steamboat industry did not blindly proceed assuming that steamers would always be the preferred choice. This was perhaps due to railroads maturing in parallel with steamer lines. In other words, the steamboats knew that they had no choice but to find a way to compete with the railroads. The railroads, in contrast, did not see the coming impact of the automobile and truck industry.

Railroads

The first reported self-propelled steam vehicle was in the late 1600s. Thus, just as with steamboats, the technology exploration process started quite early. By the late 1700s, a French-built steam car had been demonstrated in Paris. Soon after, an English-built car was demonstrated. The first practical and successful locomotive was built in Britain by John Blenkinsop in 1812.

The beginning of the railway industry is usually reported as starting with George Stephenson who created the Stockton and Darlington Railway in Britain which opened in September 1825. Soon after, it is argued, the railway era really began with the opening of the Liverpool and Manchester Railway in Britain in September 1830. As with steamboats, the maturation of railroad technology to the point of market innovation took a sizable portion of 200 years.

Interest in railroads in the US developed almost as soon as in England. In February 1827, the Baltimore and Ohio Railroad was chartered. It began operations in January 1830. The effect of this new transportation technology on stagecoaches and canal boats was felt immediately. Almost overnight, investments in the older technologies decreased in value substantially. For example, stagecoach traffic on the Providence-Boston route was effectively eliminated by 1835.

You might think that owners of stagecoach or canal boat companies should have been able to see this change coming at least five to ten years in advance. However, this was seldom the case. Railroad travel was initially viewed as noisy and dirty. Consequently, there were many who thought such travel would never be widespread. This is an archetypical symptom of a silent war situation in that competitors are acknowledged but completely discounted. However, these perceptions were very wrong as the speed advantages of rail travel were substantial, as eventually was comfort.

Alfred D. Chandler in *The Railroads* (1965) and Oliver O. Jensen in *Railroads in America* (1975) chronicle the growth of the railroad industry. Once the maturity of the technology was demonstrated, first in the UK and soon after in the US, railroad "fever" became widespread. There was an avalanche of businessmen, speculators, and hawkers of plans, proposals, and prospectuses. By the time that the financial panic of 1837 struck, there were about 200 projects underway. Many of the weaker efforts failed. But the railway era continued with abandon.

By the 1850s, the railroad's effects on the American economy were pervasive. Uniform methods of construction, grading, and bridging emerged. Much of the design of rails, locomotives, coaches, and freight cars was close to what we have today, at least in terms of appearance.

A few statistics portray the growth of the industry. In 1830, there was a bit over 20 miles of track in the US. By 1890, there were almost 170,000 miles. In 1840, there were ten locomotive manufacturers. By 1850, there were 40. In 1850, there were roughly 2,500 railway companies. By 1890, there were 30 or so. Clearly, there was much growth and many players, followed by slow growth, consolidation, and consequently just a handful of players.

Both Chandler and Jensen see the severe economic depression of the 1870s as the dividing line between these periods in American railway history. Coming out of this depression, competition had replaced growth as the dominant theme. The result was dramatic consolidation. Excessive competition in terms of rate wars and reduced revenues drove this consolidation. There were too many players, all offering the same service and, therefore, having to reduce prices to gain market share. Only the fittest – or perhaps the quickest and most savvy – survived. An example of consolidation is the Pennsylvania system whose 8,000 miles in 1893 resulted from the consolidation of more than 100 smaller railroads.

Growth and subsequent consolidation led to a variety of problems for the bigger lines also. The Santa Fe was one of the biggest lines in the country, with over 9,000 miles by 1890. The Santa Fe was bankrupt by 1893. Overexpansion in the 1880s and 1890s led to bankruptcy and reorganization for many lines. By the mid-1890s, Chandler reports, a third of the mileage in the American rail system was involved in foreclosure. Consolidation continued and by 1904 the American rail system was dominated by ten major groups. Jensen notes that by 1906 consolidations had organized two-thirds of the system into seven great and several minor systems.

With the railroads, the US began the era of big business, as briefly described in Chapter 2. Names such as Vanderbilt, Morgan, Rockefeller, Gould, Pullman, Hill, and Drew dominated the period. Political advantage and legislative concessions were sought. Stock manipulations were used to gain control of the railroads. Large corporations were created and controlled. For example, Jensen notes that at one point 11 partners in J.P. Morgan's firm held 72 directorships in 47 of the country's largest companies.

The extent of this unregulated power and control began to diminish by 1913 as government regulatory bodies and labor unions began to grow in power. Chandler observes that this period completed the creation of four institutions – large corporations, investment banking houses, regulatory commissions, and labor unions. These institutions soon became integral parts of the American economy.

While it might be imagined that this institutionalization would bring stability to the transportation industry, continued change was in store. At the time, however, the future of rail transportation looked unlimited. George Hilton portrays this outlook in "The Wrong Track" in *Invention & Technology* (1993). By the early 1900s, urban transportation had been almost completely converted from horses to electric streetcars. The next logical step seemed to be the electrification of intercity transport to fill the void between streetcars and the railroads.

Numerous "interurbans" were built and provided service between the large urban areas and smaller outlying towns and cities. Their attraction was the frequency of service which greatly exceeded the once- or twice-per-day schedule of the railroads. However, interurbans never achieved profitability, were declining by the end of World War I, and had largely disappeared by the onset of the Depression.

What had not been anticipated was the automobile. The impact of the automobile was greatly underestimated. Hilton notes that one industry executive had in 1916 predicted that "the fad feature of automobile riding will gradually wear off." Here we see another example of an archetypical symptom of the silent war situation – a known alternative was discounted. The interurbans tried to compete with automobiles by hauling freight but were soon overwhelmed by the use of trucks. To a great extent, the railroads continue to this day to face this competition.

This brief history of the railroad industry provides a compelling elaboration of the pattern of situations leading to consolidation. After a long gestation period (evolution), technology matures (crosses the chasm), and explosive market growth ensues (steady growth). Numerous players enter the market and prices plummet as they scramble, trying to gain or maintain a share of the market. This leads to financial woes, which results in many failures and mergers (consolidation) and, consequently, a dramatic decrease in the number of players. For companies facing such transitions, it is essential to be able to assess the likely course of consolidation, as well as the company's likely role – e.g., acquirer vs. acquiree – in this situation. With this understanding, you can take advantage of likely opportunities and avert potential crises.

Automobiles

The notion of a self-powered passenger vehicle has a rich history. Early experiments include those of Leonardo da Vinci and Roberto Valturio's plan for a wind carriage in 1472. There were two-masted wind carriages in the Netherlands in 1600. Belgian priest Ferdinand Verbiest created a steam-propelled carriage in China in 1678. Jacques de Vaucanson developed a carriage propelled by a large clockwork in 1748. A gas-powered vehicle was demonstrated in Paris by Isaac de Rivaz in 1807.

The first true automobile was designed by Frenchman Nicolas-Joseph Cugnot in 1769. This automobile was a steam-powered tricycle and was capable of 2.25 mph for 20 minutes. Germans Carl Benz and Gottlieb Daimler are credited with the first gasoline-engine automobile in 1885. The Daimler-Benz automobile company was founded in 1895.

In the US, George Selden filed a patent for the automobile in 1879. Charles and Frank Duryea created an American gas-powered automobile in 1892–93. The first commercially successful American-made automobile was the three-horsepower Oldsmobile in 1901. This automobile was named after Ransom Eli Olds, a pioneer in the automobile industry.

By 1898, there were 50 automobile companies. Between 1904 and 1908, 241 automobile companies went into business. Thus, we see the familiar pattern of a technology maturing over a long period and then rather suddenly, following the first successful commercialization of this technology, hundreds of companies are formed in hopes of making their fortunes with this technology. While the current situation was steady growth, the stage was already set for consolidation.

Interestingly, competition among technologies was not fully resolved at the turn of the century, as evidenced by the fact that, at that point, 40% of US automobiles were powered by steam, 38% by electricity, and 22% by gasoline. Also of interest, the automobile was not an instant success in the mass market. Henry Ford produced eight versions of his cars – models A, B, C, F, K, N, R, and S – before he was successful with the Model T in 1908. With the Model T, the mass market could now afford to own an automobile, and the chasm was crossed.

James Womack, Daniel Jones, and Daniel Roos chronicle the subsequent development of the automobile industry in *The Machine that Changed the World* (1991). They emphasize that Ford's success in producing a car for "everyman" was due to his transformation of manufacturing from centuries of craft production into the age of mass production. Forty years later, Eiji Toyoda and Taiichi Ohno in Japan transformed mass production into lean production – I return to this transformation a bit later.

The problem with craft production – despite its appealing images of hand-crafted quality products – is that it costs too much. The prices of the resulting products are too high for most people to afford. By employing extreme specialization, Ford was able to substantially reduce costs and thereby enable mass markets.

Craft production is characterized by a highly skilled workforce, extreme decentralization, general-purpose tools, and low production volumes. Since no company could exercise a monopoly over these types of resources, it was very easy to enter the automobile business in its early years. Consequently, by 1905 hundreds of companies in Western Europe and North America were producing small volumes of autos using craft techniques. The high costs of this method of production naturally resulted in high prices and an automobile market limited to the upper middle class and higher.

To lower prices so that a mass automobile market was possible, the costs of production had to be lowered. Ford's innovation created mass production by focusing on the complete and consistent interchangeability of parts and the simplicity of attaching them to each other. Interchangeability, simplicity, and ease of attachment enabled Ford to eliminate skilled fitters – the people who crafted each individual car together by forming, filing, and otherwise manipulating the idiosyncratic components of each individual car.

The impact of this innovation can be measured in terms of the average cycle time, i.e., the average time before the same operation was repeated by a particular production worker. Prior to Ford's innovation, the average cycle time was 514 minutes. With interchangeability, simplicity, and ease of attachment, the average cycle time was reduced to 2.3 minutes. In 1913, Ford added continuous-flow assembly lines and the average decreased to 1.2 minutes.

Ford also perfected the interchangeability of workers. Mass production jobs were so simplified that they only required a few minutes of training. Consequently, untrained and unskilled workers could readily fill these jobs. Of course, industrial engineers had to think through how the parts would all come together and just what each assembler would do. In this way, the engineers became the "knowledge workers" and replaced the machine shop owners and factory foremen of the earlier craft era.

The overall result of Ford's mass production was extreme centralization of control. His penchant for this type of control – centralized in himself – became a limiting factor in the growth of his company. John Staudenmaier in "Henry Ford's Big Flaw," *Invention & Technology* (1994), discusses the ways in which Ford's obsession with control tended to suffocate the successful company he had created. Fortunately, as is typical, the growth of this thriving industry did not depend on one person.

Alfred Sloan provided the next innovation. Sloan was hired by William Durant, founder of General Motors, to straighten out the enterprise that he had created by acquiring several car manufacturing companies. Sloan added professional management to Ford's basic concept. Professional financial and marketing specialists were added to the engineering specialists created by Ford. Sloan also standardized the internal systems and components of cars, further lowering costs. The overall result for the industry was a revolution in marketing and management.

Ford lured people into the routine and boring jobs of mass production with high wages – the aforementioned infamous $5 per day. The nature of these jobs caused people to focus on work conditions, including seniority and job rights in the face of cyclical auto markets. As a result, they borrowed an innovation from the railroads – job-control unionism. The combination of Ford's factory practices, Sloan's marketing and management techniques, and organized labor's control of job assignments and work tasks resulted in the final maturation of mass production.

Womack and his colleagues use this understanding of the emergence and maturation of mass production as a backdrop against which Japan's innovations in lean production are described. They emphasize the inability of Japanese culture to adapt to mass production. In particular, Japanese requirements for lifetime employment rendered impossible the large hirings and layoffs typical of mass production. Given that people were employed for life, it only made sense to invest in them so that they had multiple skills that would benefit the company.

Based on this point of view, the pioneering work of Taiichi Ohno at Toyota led to the paradigm of lean production. He began by experimenting with flat team concepts. Ohno also reconsidered the supplier-assembler relationship and decided that the goals of low cost and high quality could best be achieved by a close working relationship and long-term commitment. He also developed a new way to coordinate the flow of parts within the supply system on a day-to-day basis which is called the just-in-time system or "kanban" at Toyota. The principles of lean production were fully worked out by the 1960s. However, it took until the 1980s for the world to be at the same point in the diffusion of lean production that it was with mass production in the 1920s.

Several key organizational features are central to lean production. Design and development occur in parallel and are team-oriented in terms of communication, authority, and rewards. For production, the maximum number of tasks and responsibilities are transferred to those workers actually adding value to the car on the line. This requires learning far more professional skills than in mass production. These skills are applied creatively in this team setting rather than in a rigid hierarchy.

Another central characteristic is the incorporation of a system for detecting defects in a way that quickly traces every problem discovered to its ultimate cause. This system, in addition to the team orientation, results in the much-heralded continuous quality improvement programs of Japanese car manufacturers. This penchant for quality in particular, and lean production in general, has slowly but surely been adopted by non-Japanese car manufacturers. For example, Ford worked with Mazda, and Rover worked with Honda. Interestingly, both of these efforts were prompted by crises which are often precursors of major changes.

Womack and his colleagues visited many plants throughout the world to assess the extent to which lean production has been adopted. They note that many plants in the US have attempted to use high technology to eliminate production workers. However, they conclude that without an appropriate organization, the high-tech solution can result in adding many indirect technical and service workers, undermining any potential gain in productivity. Their visits to European auto factories sometimes led to the conclusion that the culture was still at the craft stage, even though they were trying mass production and aspiring to lean production.

They conclude their chronicle of the automobile industry by noting that Ford and Sloan built upon earlier production and management innovations in the railroad industry, as well as other industries. While they did not originate the elements of their systems, they were, nevertheless, the first to create such comprehensive systems. By 1920, mass production was broadly embraced in the US. Europe, in contrast, very reluctantly abandoned craft production. They waited until after World War II when guest workers became available who were willing to tolerate the working conditions of mass production.

Post-war Japan provided an opportunity, and perhaps a necessity, for rethinking automobile production. This situation precipitated a creative environment for Taiichi Ohno, as well as fertile ground for the concepts of thinkers such as W. Edwards Deming. As a result, the emerging dominant paradigm in the automobile industry is lean production, which Womack and his colleagues argue will be to everybody's benefit.

Reflecting on this brief history of the automobile industry, I see a few patterns. First, we yet again see versions of the consolidation situation. While there were hundreds of automobile companies in the US in the early 1900s, there are now three. A significant portion of the US automobile market has been lost to off-shore producers, but the total number of car companies is still small – say 20 or so. Thus, we see roughly 1% have survived in some form or another.

We also see examples of the silent war situation. In fact, Magaziner and Patinkin (1989) discuss the Japanese auto industry as an example of a competitor going unacknowledged until it is almost too late. In subsequent case studies, there are examples of a silent war situation where the delayed recognition of the competition was too late and it was impossible to recoup.

This chronicle also illustrates the process situation. This situation involves taking existing product innovations and adding value in terms of process innovations. The result is a higher-quality, lower-cost version of these products. While the original product innovations are likely to have created demand for these products – in other words, created the market – process innovations may take over the market. Thus, originators of product concepts do not necessarily survive to reap the benefits of mass markets. Henry Ford and Alfred Sloan proved this, as did Taiichi Ohno.

This case study also provides examples of the crossover situation. This situation involves one industry innovating by wholesale adoption of another industry's technologies and practices. We saw this with Ford and Sloan's adoption of the practices pioneered in the railroad industry and elsewhere.

Another interesting example involves the invention of the military tank. Niles White describes this process in "From Tractor to Tank" in *Invention & Technology* (1993). Benjamin Holt created the first steam traction engine – a tractor – in 1890. Faced with the problem of plowing marshland, he added tracks – a centuries-old idea – in 1904. He called the resulting vehicle a Caterpillar, which became his company's trademark in 1910. By 1916, Holt had sold 2,000 caterpillars in more than 20 countries. Thus, it took over 20 years from Holt's initial tractor until substantial business success. This is a good example of the evolution situation.

The British army, in the person of Ernest Swindon, approached Holt with the idea of creating a tracked military vehicle – the tank. Holt was uninterested in military applications. However, this did not deter Swindon who subsequently wrote Holt to thank him for proving that the technology would work so that the British army could proceed with confidence. In this way, the tracked vehicle concept crossed over from one industry to another.

In working with companies in the automobile industry, I have been struck by how very similar most cars are. Most, if not all, innovations are relatively small and are diffused throughout the industry very quickly. This situation has many of the characteristics of commodity trap situations. As a consequence, great emphasis is placed on quality control and controlling costs, as well as marketing and sales. Margins are inherently low and profits come with high sales volumes.

Why would anyone want to be in such a business? I think that the primary answer is that they are already in this business. They have made major capital investments and they have to take advantage of these commitments. Put another way, they may be organically limited from making substantial changes. I discuss this type of limitation in great detail later in this chapter in the context of the defense industry.

One strategy for extricating yourself from such a situation is to pursue multiple situations simultaneously. For example, you may have no choice but to pursue a process situation for your traditional, mainstream business. However, you can create vision quest, evolution, and crossover situations in parallel. With patience and persistence, one or more of these situations may lead to robust steady growth situations in three to five years.

Aircraft

Flight has always fascinated people. Serious speculation about flight occupied such thinkers as Roger Bacon in the thirteenth century and Leonardo da Vinci in the fifteenth century. John Wilkins in the seventeenth century forecasted the evolution of fixed-wing aircraft. During the eighteenth and nineteenth centuries, science fiction writers, including Jules Verne in France, popularized the idea of flight.

Frenchman Félix du Temple attempted, but failed, to demonstrate full-scale powered flight in 1857. Samuel Pierpont Langley demonstrated in 1901 the first flight of a heavier-than-air vehicle powered by a gasoline engine. In that year, he also tried two tests on a manned vehicle, but both ended in failure. Ironically, Langley's aircraft was later (1914) reconditioned by Glenn Curtiss and, with a few modifications, flown for brief periods.

In December 1903, Orville Wright flew for 12 seconds and landed without damage. On the fourth flight, the next day, Wilbur flew for 59 seconds covering 852 feet. The aviation era was not yet born, however. Orville and Wilbur had much marketing and sales to do yet. Finally, in 1908 they secured a government contract to build and deliver an aircraft for $25,000 (McCullough, 2016).

Thus, as with steamboats, railroads, and automobiles, the development of aircraft technology involved a long gestation period. Further, the aviation industry matured quite slowly because of the capital and risks involved. Consequently, government support was usually needed, typically in the form of military procurements or mail delivery contracts. The government faced the choice of providing this support to aviation or outright public ownership of the industry.

The government's role broadened with the formation of the National Advisory Committee for Aeronautics (NACA) in 1915. NACA later became the National Aeronautics and Space Administration (NASA). NACA was authorized to own laboratories and perform research. Their first facility was Langley Field in Virginia.

John B. Rae chronicles the development of the aviation industry in *Climb to Greatness* (1968). He begins just as World War I was emerging. In 1914 the Census Bureau listed 16 firms as aircraft manufacturers. Their combined total output for the year was 49 planes. In contrast, by 1918, the American aircraft industry was delivering 14,000 aircraft with 175,000 employees. However, after the signing of the World War I armistice, $100M in contracts were canceled in a few days. Production dropped from 14,000 in 1918 to 263 in 1922.

The strongest surviving companies included the Curtiss Aeroplane Company, Boeing Airplane Company, and Wright Aeronautical Company. The founder of the Curtiss Company was the aforementioned Glenn Curtiss. The Boeing Company was founded by William Boeing who made his first fortune in the lumber business. The Wright Aeronautical Company had been the Wright-Martin Company until Glen Martin left in 1917. Wright-Martin had emerged from the sale of the Wright Company (formed by the Wright brothers) to Martin in 1915.

Several companies were founded in the 1920s. Douglas Aircraft was formed by Donald Douglas, a former chief engineer for Glenn Martin. Sikorsky Aero Engineering Corporation was founded by Igor Sikorsky. Pratt & Whitney was formed by Frederick Rentschler. Lockheed was founded by the Loughead brothers. Other new companies included Detroit Aircraft (which eventually owned 87% of Lockheed), Grumman Aircraft, AVCO (Aviation Corporation), Fairchild Engine and Airplane Company, and Ryan Aeronautical Company.

As of 1925, California had four aircraft companies and New York had 15. Soon after, Charles Lindbergh's solo flight across the Atlantic in 1927 sold the American people on commercial aviation. The chasm was crossed and there were 300 aircraft factories by 1928.

Thus, the aircraft industry was booming, at least in terms of new companies, if not profits. Many of the company names that we now view as synonymous with aviation were in business during this steady growth situation. Many others, which few of us recall, were formed but disappeared.

With the increasing maturity of the industry, aircraft manufacturers began to think in terms of vertical integration, including operating their own airlines and building their own airframes, engines, and components.

For example, Boeing reorganized as the United Aircraft and Transportation Company in 1929. With such developments, the possibility emerged that a few large companies would completely dominate the industry.

The Air Mail Act of 1934 ended this possibility. In compliance with this legislation, United separated into three segments. Boeing again became the Boeing Airplane Company. The airline subsidiaries became United Airlines. The eastern manufacturing divisions – Pratt & Whitney, Hamilton Standard, Chance Vought, and Sikorsky – became the United Aircraft Corporation.

North American and AVCO followed the same general pattern. North American was reconstituted as a manufacturing concern and its airlines were organized into two companies, Transcontinental and Western (TWA) and Eastern. AVCO's aircraft manufacturing divisions became the Aviation Manufacturing Corporation and its transport company emerged as American Airlines.

Commercial aviation in the 1930s was dominated by Douglas Aircraft's DC-3. Within two years of its introduction, Douglas had sold more than 800 and DC-3s were carrying 95% of the nation's civil air traffic. For military aircraft, only about a dozen companies competed. Four airframe manufacturers (Douglas, Boeing, Curtiss-Wright, and North American) and two engine manufacturers (Curtiss-Wright and Pratt & Whitney) dominated.

However, there were still new entries, in part due to quickly changing technologies for airframes, wings, propellers, and landing gear. When United Aircraft and Transport decided to move its Avion subsidiary (founded by John K. Northrop) to Wichita, Northrop left United to form Northrop Corporation because he wanted to stay in Los Angeles. Douglas Aircraft owned half the stock of this new company. Other companies formed in this period included the Seversky Aircraft Corporation (later Republic Aviation Corporation), Beech Aircraft Corporation, Bell Aircraft Corporation, Piper Aircraft Corporation, and McDonnell Aircraft Corporation. Consolidated Aircraft in San Diego became Convair.

Despite the growth in the number of players in the industry, companies were still very dependent on military orders to avoid a crisis. Not until the closing days of the 1930s, with war looming, were even the major firms secure. With the onset of World War II, aircraft production soared. However, by the end of 1945 contracts valued at over $21 billion were canceled, and only 16 aircraft plants remained in operation out of 66 that had been functioning a year earlier.

Four of the five large West Coast companies – Boeing, Douglas, Lockheed, and North American – emerged from the war in reasonably strong positions. Convair, in contrast, was not in good shape. While the prices of aircraft had increased very substantially over a 15-year period, from $50,000 for the Boeing 247 to $1,250,000 for the Boeing 377, aircraft companies were still losing money.

The Finletter Commission in 1947 analyzed the problems of the aircraft industry and concluded, among other things, that problems included government-dominated demand which fluctuated violently leading to a lack of production continuity which undermined maintaining a workforce. They also noted that the industry was characterized by high engineering costs, extremely long manufacturing cycles, and quick obsolescence.

By 1949 six West Coast airframe companies – Boeing, Convair, Douglas, Lockheed, North American, and Northrop – had 69% of the total dollar value of military orders. Only two newcomers – McDonnell and Beech – were among the top 16 aircraft manufacturers. Thus, consolidation continued unabated, as it has continued to this day. For example, in the 1990s, Lockheed bought General Dynamics' aircraft operations, Northrop bought Grumman, and Lockheed and Martin-Marietta merged.

In 1949, Glenn Martin, a great pioneer in aviation, left the Martin Company. By 1953, the Martin Company was effectively out of the airframe business. In 1954, Chance Vought was separated from United Aircraft. Later in the 50s, General Dynamics bought Convair.

As late as 1958, over half of the commercial aircraft in the world were built by Douglas, having continually built upon the success of the DC-3. However, Boeing quickly moved into jet aircraft, mostly due to military contracts. Using the military KC-135 as a starting point, Boeing introduced the 707 commercial transport in 1958. Douglas was much slower to shift paradigms, and the DC-8 did not appear until 1959. Boeing's "bet" on jet aircraft provided the basis for its strong position in commercial aviation today.

The 1960s saw many mergers and continued consolidation. Textron acquired the Bell Aerospace Corporation. Vought and its Dallas neighbors merged to form Ling-Temco-Vought in 1961. Temco – Texas Engineering and Manufacturing Company – was founded in 1945. Also in 1961, the Martin Company expanded beyond the aerospace field by merging with the Marietta Corporation, a manufacturer of cement, lime, and rock products as well as chemicals. The resulting company became the Martin-Marietta

Corporation, which in the 1990s acquired several military electronics firms and then, as noted earlier, merged with Lockheed.

In 1967, North American merged with Rockwell-Standard to become North American Rockwell Corporation. Also in 1967, Douglas merged with McDonnell to become McDonnell-Douglas Corporation. Such consolidation became necessary so that the resulting few large concerns could withstand the feast-and-famine cycle typical of the industry. By the 1990s, three airframe manufacturers controlled the commercial aircraft industry including a dominant Boeing, a heavily subsidized Airbus, and a very much weakened Douglas. Similarly, a few avionics companies dominated, as did three aircraft engine companies. Consolidation seemed to be nearly complete.

Beyond the compelling example of consolidation situations illustrated by this chronicle of the aircraft industry, there are several other types of situations that are interesting to elaborate on. T.A. Heppenheimer in "The Dream of the Flying Wing," *Invention & Technology* (1994), tells of John K. Northrop's fascination with the possibility of a flying wing. Unlike a typical aircraft whose wings are attached to its fuselage, a flying wing is an aircraft that is basically all wing.

Jack Northrop was born in 1895. By the time he was 20 years old, he was a regular visitor at the auto and airplane shop of Allan and Malcolm Loughhead. Northrop's first aircraft design was the Loughhead S-1. Unfortunately, the post-war economy led to few contracts, and Loughhead folded in 1920.

Northrop joined Donald Douglas in 1923. Working in his spare time, Northrop developed what was to become the Vega. He went to work for a rejuvenated Loughhead – now Lockheed – in 1926 and the first Vega emerged in mid-1927. It was a big hit, providing Northrop with a little freedom.

He now focused on the flying wing. While the concept of a flying wing was not new, no one had ever built one. Allan Loughhead would not back him. Consequently, he started a new company, the Avion Corporation, with the backing of the Hearst publishing family. There was a demonstration flight in 1930.

The Depression hit and Boeing bought out Avion in 1931. Boeing decided to move this operation to Wichita, Kansas. As mentioned earlier, Northrop did not want to move to the midwest. He left to join Douglas in a joint venture, and participated in the DC-2 and DC-3. Douglas bought him out in 1937, the proceeds of which led to the creation of the Northrop Corporation with, as noted earlier, Douglas as a shareholder.

Northrop's next flying wing took to the air in 1940–41. He subsequently won a contract during World War II to build a bomber (B-35) using this concept which was flight tested in 1946. His competition – the B-36 – was canceled in 1948 and he won a contract to build 30 B-49s, a jet-powered version of the B-35. However, contract negotiations broke down when he would not agree to build the B-49 in Texas. Consequently, the B-36 was resuscitated.

Efforts to save the B-49 floundered on technical arguments. The flying wing, it was argued, was too heavy and created too much drag at high speeds. In late 1949, the order came to scrap the 11 existing B-49s. Northrop soon after got a contract to produce the F-89 fighter. Heppenheimer reports that Northrop was nevertheless crushed and never got over it.

This story ends in 1980. Northrop, now old and feeble in a wheelchair, saw the blueprints for the B-2 stealth bomber. The stealthy properties of the flying wing – which Northrop had not foreseen – had vindicated Northrop's vision. Of particular interest to our discussion, it is important to note that it took over 50 years for his vision to be realized.

Curt Wohleber discusses a similar story in "Straight Up," *Invention & Technology* (1993). This is the story of Igor Sikorsky's vision of the helicopter. He built his first prototype helicopters in 1909 and 1910 while still in Russia. He then shifted his attention to fixed-wing aircraft, first in Russia and subsequently in the US where, as noted earlier, he formed the Sikorsky Aero Engineering Corporation. His company later became a division of United Aircraft.

In 1938, he proposed to United Aircraft that a helicopter be built. The first test flight of his VS-300 occurred in September, 1939 when Sikorsky was 50. (VS stood for Vought-Sikorsky due to the merger of United Aircraft's Sikorsky and Chance Vought divisions.) While the VS-300 was great at hovering, it unfortunately was not good at forward motion, especially straight forward.

His next helicopter was the XR-4, a military prototype. By the end of World War II, 400 R-4, R-5, and R-6 helicopters had been produced. However, commercial use was slow to come and it took quite a few years before helicopters were commonly used for other than military purposes. It took over 30 years for Sikorsky to realize his vision, and over 40 until this vision resulted in business success.

The stories of Jack Northrop and Igor Sikorsky are similar in that it took several decades for their visions to be realized. This certainly qualifies their stories as examples of evolution situations. In particular, these stories epitomize the slow maturation of technology from initial visions to commercial viability.

These stories also provide exemplars of vision quest situations. This type of situation involves an individual, or occasionally a team, persisting over a very long period of time to make a dream come true. Often, they are way ahead of their times in that technologies necessary to realize their dream may not yet be available. This may deter them for a period, but they eventually return to pursue their dreams. Many, if not most, dreams are never fulfilled. However, this possibility does not seem to occur to those on vision quests.

There are also examples of the silent war situation in this case study of the aviation industry. One of these is chronicled by T.A. Heppenheimer in "The Jet Plane is Born," *Invention & Technology* (1993). Going into World War II, other countries could not compete with US aircraft engine technology. America's piston-driven airplanes were far superior due to the turbocharger, which enabled American planes to achieve unprecedented altitudes and speeds.

Rather than attempt to catch up, the English and Germans turned to the unproven idea of jets. The Americans, snug in their advantage, discounted the potential of jet engines. Thus, a big advantage almost became a very big disadvantage and America was nearly left behind. Collaboration with the English during World War II fortunately enabled the US to catch up.

This vignette epitomizes the silent war situation in that the victim of the competition does not even realize that competition is happening. They may be aware of the competing technology, but they have completely discounted its potential. Thus, they sit by and unknowingly provide few if any barriers to the success of their competitors.

A contemporary version of the silent war situation involves Airbus, the aforementioned government-sponsored European consortium of English, French, German, and Spanish aircraft companies. Airbus has succeeded in becoming second in the commercial aircraft market, displacing McDonnell-Douglas which was acquired by Boeing. Airbus and Boeing remain the only competitors and constantly compare scorecards in terms of orders booked and aircraft delivered.

However, Boeing faces the disadvantage of the US government not being willing to provide the types of support provided by the European governments. While the US government provides military development contracts, as well as aviation R&D funding via agencies such as National Aeronautics and Space Administration (NASA), it does not become directly involved with issues such as financing of airlines' purchases of US-built commercial aircraft. In this way, there is a silent war because the potential victim has apparently discounted the impacts of one or more key competitive advantages of the adversary.

I have been involved with the aviation industry for many years, initially in R&D but more recently on the business side of this industry. For example, I have chaired a couple of long-range planning committees that focused on technology trends and potential operational problems. I have also conducted numerous planning workshops and projects for aircraft and avionics companies. I served on an advisory committee for Boeing that focused on evaluating the cockpit design for the new Boeing 777 aircraft. These experiences led me to suggest the following prospects for this industry.

As is readily apparent from the discussion in this section, this industry has gone through a tremendous amount of consolidation. There are only a handful of players and they all know each other very well. Substantial effort is invested in trying to differentiate their offerings in terms of performance, economy, and safety.

However, there is a dilemma which is characterized by the industry saying, "You spend money in the cockpit, save money in maintenance, and make money in the cabin." In other words, you spend money to assure performance, economy, and safety and try to meet all maintenance requirements as economically as possible. However, you can only make money by satisfying passengers.

From passengers' perspectives, all the airplanes are pretty much the same. What matters is comfort, service, and price. Further, business passengers – who provide most of the profits – increasingly want "office in the sky" capabilities such as telephone, computer, email connectivity, and so on. This trend led me, during one of my planning workshops with an aircraft company, to suggest that the winners in the airline competition would be the ones that provide the best information technology to passengers. The aircraft itself would become, in effect, a computer cabinet and not the essence of the value added to the industry.

While this once would have seemed outlandish, it was taken very seriously. The aircraft could become, in effect, a commodity such as

I discussed for automobiles. The profit margins would then be greatest for those providing the information technology. For the aircraft manufacturers, a dearly held paradigm would then be lost and they would find themselves in a commodity trap situation.

This scenario has already emerged. The organic nature of aircraft companies and their huge capital investments may necessitate that they simply accept this fate. In fact, this possibility was acknowledged by a Boeing executive in the industry magazine *Interavia* (1994). If aircraft companies take such scenarios seriously, they may be able to avoid many of the snares in the commodity trap.

Summary

The case studies of innovation in the steamboat, railroad, automobile, and aircraft industries have greatly enriched our understanding of the common situations experienced. The chronicles of each of these industries provide ample support and elaboration of the evolution situation. The technologies underlying these industries all took a very long time to mature – on the order of 100 to 200 years.

These technologies were, nevertheless, viewed as revolutionary at the time of their relatively sudden market success. Similarly, we now view information technologies as revolutionary. The revolution is in terms of the impact of these technologies on our lives, not in terms of the emergence of the technologies. In this way, every era has its "high-tech" trends and events. We are not unique in being challenged by these types of changes.

As noted earlier, I find it very easy to imagine the atmosphere surrounding the development of steamboats in the early 1800s, railroads in the mid-1800s, automobiles at the turn of the century, and aircraft in the early 1900s. I am sure that the pioneers and entrepreneurs in these industries keenly felt the exhilaration of change and competition. Their stories of change affected them as substantially as current stories are affecting us.

The case studies in this section also contain numerous examples of the silent war situation. These examples include the impact of the railroads on stagecoaches and canal boats, the effects of automobiles on railroads and particularly the interurbans, the innovations of Japanese automobile manufacturers relative to those in the US and Europe, the potentially preemptive challenge of the English and German jet engines against smug US manufacturers of piston engines, and the impact of government-sponsored Airbus on Boeing and Douglas. In all of these examples, we see industry leaders calmly enjoying their perches while often acknowledged, but usually discounted, competitors take away their markets.

This section also provided many examples of the consolidation situation. Opportunity emerges and companies proliferate. Overexpansion results in price cutting to gain market share. Profits disappear. The industry then consolidates to include a few dominant players who mature and often become institutionalized. This situation has been dramatically played out in all of the industries discussed in this book.

There were also examples of the process situation. Ford and Sloan innovated in terms of process changes in the automobile industry, as did Ohno more recently. The crossover situation was illustrated by Ford and Sloan's borrowing many of their innovations from the railroad industry and elsewhere. Another example of crossover is the military adoption of the tracked vehicle concept from the farm machinery and heavy equipment industry. Crossover involves seeing connections rather than creating technologies.

There were also several examples of the vision quest. Northrop's vision of the flying wing and Sikorsky's vision of the helicopter are primary examples. Ford's vision of the mass market for automobiles – realized on his ninth attempt – is another example. Holt's vision of tracked vehicles is yet another illustration.

The vision quest is interesting in that it illustrates the effects that men and women can have on their times, in contrast to the effects that their times have on them. The vision quest proceeds even when the times are not ready. Patience, persistence, and often passion drive people to overcome obstacles and eventually succeed. While this situation seems quite positive – perhaps even uplifting – it also has drawbacks, not the least of which may be decades of business failure until success eventually emerges.

To conclude this section, consider the distinction between organic and synthetic perspectives of how organizations anticipate, recognize, and respond to change. The case studies in this chapter have illustrated many attempts to synthesize new organizations in response to the organic processes of consolidation. However, because we focused on industry segments as wholes, rather than individual companies, it is difficult to determine how the enterprises noted balanced organic and synthetic perspectives.

EXPLOITATIONS BY TRANSPORTATION

Innovations in transportation transformed society. Economic growth resulted. The US Department of Transportation estimates that transportation and transportation-related industries employ over 13.3 million people, accounting for 9.1% of workers in the United States. Employment in these industries rose steadily from 2011 to 2015 to 13.6 million, exceeding prerecession levels, then declined to 13.3 million in 2017.

The Bureau of Transportation Statistics reported that transportation services (for-hire, in-house, and household) contributed $1.3 trillion (5.6%) to an enhanced US gross domestic product (GDP) of $23.7 trillion in 2021 – as measured by the Bureau of Transportation Statistics' Transportation Satellite Accounts. To put this in perspective, agriculture accounted for 11.9% of GDP, industry 17.7%, and services 70.4%.

This growth resulted in a range of exploitations, summarized in Table 3.2. Exploitation via "externalities" concerns societal impacts for which manufacturers and service providers are not accountable:

- Vehicles pollute, affecting health due to air quality
- Vehicles' carbon emissions contribute to global warming
- Vehicle accidents injure and kill people
- Discarded tires and vehicles clog landfills

Exploiters focus on maximizing efficiency and profits at the expense of environment, health, and safety. A human-centered society creates mechanisms to counter these tendencies.

TABLE 3.2

Innovation and Exploitation in Transportation

Innovations	Ships, railroads, automobiles, and airplanes.
Financial exploitation	Monopoly pricing, depressed wages, waste, fraud, and abuse.
Physical exploitation	Air pollution, noise pollution, carbon emissions, and accident injuries.
Psychological exploitation	Traffic stress, traveling stress, and needless worry.
Mitigating exploitation	Regulations, anti-trust laws, and externality taxes.

In this section, I address exploitation by vehicle manufacturers and vehicle service providers. In a later section, I discuss exploitation by the Defense Industrial Base – Lockheed, Raytheon, Boeing, Northrup, General Dynamics – and the broader Military Industrial Complex with close links among defense contractors, the Pentagon, and politicians.

Financial Exploitation

Automobile companies are making record profits on some vehicles. The average price of a new vehicle in the US now exceeds $50,000 (DePillis & Smialek, 2023). I bought a Toyota Tacoma in 2011 for $18,000. This vehicle now sells for $50,000. The price has increased by 9% per year for 12 years.

General Motors earns a $17,000 average profit on each pickup truck it sells. Large sport utility vehicles (SUVs) have similar profit margins. A portion of these cash flows is used to subsidize low-end vehicles in order to meet Corporate Average Fuel Economy (CAFÉ) standards for light-duty vehicles. Trucks and large SUVs are not subject to these standards.

Ferrari S.p.A., an Italian luxury sports car manufacturer based in Maranello, Italy, has perhaps the current record for profitability. The profit on each Ferrari car sold exceeds $100,000. Of course, we need to keep in mind, that whether it is a Ferrari, large SUV, or pickup truck, consumers are able to decide whether or not to be financially exploited.

Physical Exploitation

In this section, I consider CO_2 emissions and air pollution due to transportation, the physical impacts of vehicles on lives and space utilizations, and the transformation of the automobile industry as we move from fossil fuel internal combustion engines to battery electric vehicles.

CO_2 Emissions

The Environmental Protection Agency (2023) publishes an *Inventory of US Greenhouse Gas Emissions and Sinks*. Sources of emissions by sector include:

- Transportation, 28%
- Electric power, 25%

- Industry, 23%
- Commercial and residential, 13%
- Agriculture, 10%

Within transportation, the sources are:

- Light-duty vehicles, 58%
- Medium and heavy-duty trucks, 23%
- Aircraft, 8%
- Other, 6% (buses, motorcycles, pipelines, and lubricants)
- Ships and boats, 3%
- Rail, 2%

They report that

> A typical passenger vehicle emits about 4.6 metric tons of carbon dioxide per year. This assumes the average gasoline vehicle on the road today has a fuel economy of about 22.0 miles per gallon and drives around 11,500 miles per year. Every gallon of gasoline burned creates about 8,887 grams of CO_2.

> This amounts to 20 pounds per gallon of gas, which weighs about six pounds. How can this happen? Gasoline is about 87% carbon and 13% hydrogen by weight. So the carbon in a gallon of gasoline (weighing 6.3 pounds) weighs 5.5 pounds (0.87×6.3 pounds = 5.5 pounds). So, multiply the weight of the carbon times 3.7, which equals 20 pounds of carbon dioxide! Most of the weight of the CO_2 does not come from the gasoline itself, but from the oxygen in the air.

> The Environmental Protection Agency (EPA) also reports that CO_2 emissions from commercial aviation averages 142 grams of CO_2 per seat per mile. At a cruising speed of 780 km per hour, this is equivalent to 90 kg of CO_2 per passenger per hour.

Air Pollution

Fuller and colleagues (2022) report that

> Pollution remains responsible for approximately nine million deaths per year, corresponding to one in six deaths worldwide. Reductions have occurred in the number of deaths attributable to the types of pollution associated with extreme poverty. However, these reductions in deaths

from household air pollution and water pollution are offset by increased deaths attributable to ambient air pollution and toxic chemical pollution (i.e., lead). Deaths from these modern pollution risk factors, which are the unintended consequence of industrialization and urbanization, have risen by 7% since 2015 and by over 66% since 2000.

Pollution – i.e., unwanted waste of human origin released to air, land, water, and the ocean without regard for cost or consequence – is an existential threat to human health and planetary health, and jeopardizes the sustainability of modern societies. Pollution includes contamination of air by fine particulate matter; ozone; oxides of sulfur and nitrogen; freshwater pollution; contamination of the ocean by mercury, nitrogen, phosphorus, plastic, and petroleum waste; and poisoning of the land by lead, mercury, pesticides, industrial chemicals, electronic waste, and radioactive waste.

Pollutants that contribute to poor air quality include particulate matter (PM), nitrogen oxides (NOx), and volatile organic compounds (VOCs). The transportation sector is responsible for approximately 45% of NOx total emissions inventory in the US and less than 10% of VOC emissions in the US.

Impacts of Vehicles

The Centers for Disease Prevention and Control (2022) reports that each year, 1.35 million people are killed on roadways around the world. Every day, almost 3,700 people are killed globally in crashes involving cars, buses, motorcycles, bicycles, trucks, or pedestrians. An average of 36,791 crash deaths occurred each year (101 deaths each day) during 2015–2019 in the United States.

In 2019, the population-based death rate in the US (11.1 per 100,000 population; 36,355 deaths) was the highest among the 29 high-income countries and was 2.3 times the average rate of the 28 other high-income countries. The population-based death rate in the US increased by 0.1% from 2015 to 2019, whereas the average change among 27 other high-income countries was 10.4%.

This reflects the simple fact that streets are designed for the efficiency of vehicle transit rather than the safety of pedestrians.

When suburbs were new, (streets and roads) were considered efficient solutions, not problems. They moved traffic efficiently across sprawling distances. In 1929, the *New York Times* wrote of the benefit that a 'magnificent artery of traffic' in wide, straight roads would provide in speeding traffic through Nassau and Suffolk counties. Now, safe-street advocates say (streets and roads) are inhospitable to anything other than motor vehicles.

(Negroni, 2023)

An enormous amount of space is devoted to parking, mandated by city building ordinances.

Approximately 2 billion parking spots cover the country, enough to pave over the entire state of Connecticut. From baseball stadiums in Los Angeles to malls in Atlanta, parking lots are bigger than the buildings they surround. Cities have built so much parking through a policy few people know: minimum parking requirements. Cities don't just require parking spaces for nearly every office, mall, store, movie theater, bowling alley, restaurant and other building, those requirements often include a certain number of spots for every building.

(Myersohn, 2023)

The cost of creating a parking space is $26,000 per space nationally; and $36,000 in Manhattan, not counting the cost of land.

Baker (2023) provides an insightful review of Daniel Knowles' recent book *Carmageddon: How Cars Make Life Worse and What to Do About It* (Knowles, 2023). He reports that Knowles

shows how they pollute the air, inefficiently consume enormous amounts of natural resources, take up too much space, and kill and injure too many people. They make cities into worse places: less pleasant, less walkable and bikeable, harder to enjoy, dirtier, and louder. They stress us out and make our lives more sedentary. We need, Knowles argues, to get as many of them off the road as we can, as quickly as possible.

The challenge now, for transit as for so many other issues, is not to identify the best policies but to figure out how they might be implemented on the rough terrain of politics. That is: Who benefits from widespread car dependence today, and how can these beneficiaries' positions be weakened? What existing coalitions might be willing to fight these battles, what new coalitions will be needed and how might they be formed? Once formed, how might those coalitions actually win?

Industry Transformation

All of the above is playing out as the automobile industry is having to entertain fundamental transformation. The industry is having to change, driven by electrification, which has enabled new entrants. "Everything about carmaking is changing at once" (Wright, 2023). Auto companies will inevitably have to deal with enormous changes – technically, behaviorally, and socially (Laczkowski et al., 2023).

Wright provides this assessment:

> In future, car brands will be differentiated mainly by the experience of using them, which is now determined more by their software than their hardware. Software-defined vehicles, which nowadays resemble supercomputers on wheels, will have ever more features and functions such as infotainment, ambient lighting, and voice controls, all improved by over-the-air (OTA) updates after a vehicle has left the factory. That will open up new ways for the car producers to cash in.
>
> The race to autonomous self-driving is also on. Though the road to fully autonomous cars is littered with obstacles, a more limited "hands-off" autonomy that takes over driving duties initially on motorways and eventually in some urban settings is close to commercial deployment. Carmakers are rethinking their involvement in ride-hailing and car sharing, with the big question over mobility becoming how best to monetize the use rather than the mere ownership of cars, triggering a rethink of car retailing.
>
> A final test comes from new geopolitical tensions, notably between America and China. Rising tariffs, growing restrictions on tech transfers, a reshoring of supply chains, and greater subsidies for home-grown manufacturing all threaten to halt or even reverse the process of globalization. Carmakers will find adjusting to such a change especially challenging.
>
> For legacy firms all this requires big change and re-engineering. They retain many advantages: skills in manufacturing, powerful brands, and access to massive amounts of capital in an industry that eats through it. However, startups are not weighed down by the heavy legacy of siloed organizations that have for decades been dedicated to mechanical engineering and are encumbered by a complex portfolio of products that heap on costs. Not all legacy firms will survive the coming transformation.

The Economist characterizes the evolving situation.

> Autonomous driving should eventually change long car journeys from a chore to a better use of time. For carmakers it will be a way to make money from supplying the systems. More free time in cars should also create opportunities to sell new features such as upgraded infotainment and services such as streaming music and films. The new approach to mobility is one more sign of a switch from ownership to usership.
>
> **(The Economist, 2023a)**

The MIT Mobility Initiative is providing a platform to address the merger of public, private, and academic spheres to help shape the future of transportation (Shulman, 2023).

> Few sectors of the global economy are changing as rapidly and dramatically as the mobility sector, and even fewer have mobility's broad potential to shape the way we live. New technologies are upending long-static industries such as automobile manufacturing and highway construction, and altering the way we plan our cities and homes. The climate crisis is compelling the mobility and transportation industries to innovate in ways that are not only new but also clean and sustainable.

Psychological Exploitation

Driving can be a relaxing, enjoyable journey on an open road on a beautiful day, but not always. Being stuck in traffic tends to be frustrating and time consuming. "In DC, Los Angeles, and San Francisco, the typical car commuter spends more than 60 hours – more than a week of work-time per year – sitting in his car, stuck" (Werbach, 2013).

Anger and aggression can result.

> Environmental factors such as crowded roads can boost anger behind the wheel. Certain psychological factors, including displaced anger and high life stress, are also linked to road rage. In addition, studies have found that people who experience road rage are more likely to misuse alcohol and drugs.
>
> **(APA, 2014)**

Of course, alcohol and drugs are significant contributors to the 37,000 annual deaths on US roads. 30% of all highway-related deaths in the US are attributable to alcohol and drugs. According to the CDC, this amounts to one death every 45 minutes (CDC, 2023).

DEFENSE INDUSTRY

Innovations in transportation benefitted the defense industry. In fact defense markets often sustained the aviation industry (Bright, 1978). Space does not allow elaboration of the defense industry and its many innovations. However, it is useful to elaborate on how defense companies, despite enormous consolidation, have been able to avoid the typical consequences of intense competition and exploit the taxpayers' pocketbooks.

Major defense contractors enjoy monopoly positions on platforms, e.g., Lockheed Martin and the F-35. While profits may be capitated, steadily growing costs are reimbursed. Consequently, the prices of weapon systems have soared.

A recent report on 60 Minutes (CBS, 2023) interviewed former defense officials who reported, "The roots of the (price gouging) problem can be traced to 1993, when the Pentagon, looking to cut costs, urged defense companies to merge. Fifty one major contractors consolidated to five giants." Pentagon analysts found 12–15% negotiated profits have risen, in effect, to 40%.

For example,

> In the competitive environment before the companies consolidated, a shoulder fired stinger missile cost $25,000 in 1991. With Raytheon now the sole supplier, it costs more than $400,000 to replace each missile sent to Ukraine…even accounting for inflation and some improvements, that's a seven-fold increase.

The consolidation noted above was motivated by a meeting convened by Deputy Secretary of Defense William Perry, in 1993,

> At an event now referred to as 'the last supper,' Perry urged them to combine into a few, larger companies because Pentagon budget cuts would

endanger at least half the combat jet firms, missile makers, satellite builders and other contractors represented at the dinner that night.

Now the top three defense contractors have over half (51%) of the market. Norm Augustine parodied this trend in Augustine's Laws (1984).

In the year 2054, the entire defense budget will purchase just one tactical aircraft. This aircraft will have to be shared by the Air Force and Navy 3½ days each per week except for leap year, when it will be made available to the Marines for the extra day.

There are also Congressional pressures on job retention. Consequentially, production and operations are sustained whether or not platforms are needed. I elaborate on examples below. Revolving doors between government and industry employment exacerbate this phenomenon.

Defense Acquisition Reform

The factors just outlined have prompted regular attempts to reform defense acquisition laws, regulations, and processes (Levine, 2020). The most well-known of these many attempts was the President's Blue Ribbon Commission on Defense Management, informally known as the Packard Commission, which was commissioned by President Ronald Reagan in 1986. The Commission Report was issued later that year (Packard, 1986).

The acquisition process is highly multifaceted. It is infused with disparate goals and objectives: to have the highest performing technology at the lowest price possible in the fastest amount of time; to ensure the defense industry and related economies remain solvent; and to encourage small businesses, minority contractors, and women-owned businesses (Cancian, 1995).

Historically, reforms have been enacted for primarily two reasons: increasing complexity of the technologies involved and individual corruption and abuse for monetary gain. Excesses in time and cost, or deficits in performance, are some of the more obvious outward signs that reform is warranted. But these are just symptoms, and it is instructive to elucidate the contributing factors. First, is the government acquiring the right systems to meet its needs, and second, is it acquiring those systems well?

The first question addresses the agility of the acquisition enterprise. In an ever-changing world, the actions of both adversaries and allies can alter the efficacy of military systems both deployed and under development with little warning. Consequently, a program could be run with perfect efficiency and achieve all of its performance objectives, yet the resulting systems could be useless upon completion. While this does not constitute a failure in the traditional sense, a lack of agility in the acquisition system means that resources continue to be expended on a program even after it is recognized that it is no longer viable.

The second question addresses the efficiency of the acquisition process. That is, assuming that the mission is sound, does the acquisition enterprise deliver systems in the most cost-effective way possible? This category includes most of the issues one typically associates with acquisition failings including excessive oversight, lack of competition, political interference, requirements creep, and the inclusion of immature technologies. Issues with acquisition efficiency are linked to the structure of the acquisition process as well as the discipline with which the process is implemented.

Boot (2023) recently reported

For all of (the Army's) brave talk of innovation, it remains part of one of the world's biggest bureaucracies the Defense Department. It can develop weapons, but it can't acquire them in bulk; that's the job of the Pentagon's lumbering acquisitions bureaucracy. So it remains to be seen how success-ful this five-year-old command will be in speeding up the Army's innova-tion metabolism. But you have to give the Army credit for at least trying to be better prepared for war in the future than it has been in the past.

With acquisition, it is sometimes difficult to define a failure since even troubled programs often result in the acquisition of something. However, in hindsight at least, it is not always the case that the right weapon was acquired to address the right threat. Further, the costs of acquired systems often far exceed original projections, and the desired capability is often provided much later than originally planned. These are the factors that determine the effectiveness of acquisition. History has shown that not all acquisition efforts are successful with regard to these factors. These phenomena can be better illustrated by providing some examples.

Loss of Mission

This occurs when the threat that was to have been addressed by the system is no longer viable, or a new type of threat emerges. One such example is the B-70 Valkyrie. The Valkyrie was intended to be a high-altitude Mach 3+ strategic bomber. However, concerns over the aircraft's vulnerability to surface-to-air missiles as well as the increasing dominance of Intercontinental Ballistic Missiles (ICBMs) in the nuclear strike role led both the Eisenhower and Kennedy administrations to question its military viability. Eventually, the program was transformed into a research program, the XB-70.

Another example of loss of mission is the Drone Anti Submarine Helicopter (DASH). It was originally developed as an expendable anti-submarine platform. However, since submarines were not a significant threat during the Vietnam War, the DASH program was canceled in 1969. Both of these examples illustrate a lack of agility in the acquisition process in that resources were redeployed long after the changing threat had been identified.

Quite recently, Lipton (2023) reports another example of mission loss leading to wasteful spending.

Eight of the ten Freedom-class littoral combat ships now based in Jacksonville and another based in San Diego would be retired, even though they averaged only four years old and had been built to last 25 years. The Navy estimated that the move would save $4.3 billion over the next five years. Then the lobbying started. Early decommissioning of littoral combat ships at Mayport Naval Station would result in the loss of more than 2,000 direct jobs in Jacksonville," a coalition of business leaders from the Florida city wrote last summer. Within weeks, lawmakers offered amendments to the 2023 Pentagon spending authorization law that prohibited the Navy from retiring four of the eight ships in Jacksonville and the one in San Diego.

Process Failure

This can cause the cancelation of programs as well. For example, the M247 Sergeant York DIVAD (Division Air Defense gun) was born of the Army's need for a replacement for the ageing M163 20mm Vulcan A/A gun and M48 Chaparral missile system. Despite the fact that the system utilized as much off-the-shelf technology as possible, when the first production vehicles were delivered in late 1983 there were many performance deficits, including issues with the fire control system, clutter handling, turret traverse rate, and ECCM suite. Consequently, in December 1986 after about 50 vehicles had been produced, the entire program was terminated.

Of course, most acquisition process problems do not lead to cancelation. Many acquisition programs deliver highly capable systems, but only after delays and cost overruns. An example of such is the F-22 Raptor. Considered one of the most technologically advanced aircraft in the world, it is also one of the most expensive. The program began with the award of the Advanced Tactical Fighter Demonstration/Validation contract in 1986 and achieved Initial Operational Capability in 2005. The inclusion of many advanced technologies such as advanced avionics and low-observable materials helped contribute to the long duration and high cost of the program.

These and many other instances have driven desires for acquisition reform. However, past reform efforts have been less than fully successful, as shown by Drezner and colleagues (1993). Drezner reported that reform initiatives from 1960 to 1990 did not reduce cost growth on 197 defense programs. In fact, the average cost growth on these programs was 20% and did not change significantly for 30 years. Christensen and colleagues (1999) reaffirmed this conclusion and also found that initiatives based on the specific recommendations of the Packard Commission did not reduce the average cost overrun experienced (as a percentage of costs) on 269 completed defense acquisition contracts evaluated over an eight-year period (1988–1995). Actually, the cost performance experienced on development contracts and contracts managed by the Air Force worsened significantly.

Roughly ten years after the Packard Commission Report was published, the Secretary of Defense, William J. Perry, ordered the Department of Defense (DoD) to adopt many of the commercial practices recommended by the Commission. This is a good illustration of the roles that top leadership and champions play in advocating fundamental change.

The lack of reform success can, in part, be attributed to one or more of the causes discussed above. Since the 1980s, the military threat has changed from full-scale thermonuclear war to domestic terrorism, information warfare, and asymmetric warfare. Not only are weapons programs designed for a Cold War threat not always appropriate, but the entire system of acquisition has become too slow to adapt to emerging threats. The rate of technological change has advanced so rapidly that weapon systems can become obsolete before they leave the design stage. In response, the DoD has attempted large-scale, fundamental change in all facets of its operation.

The DoD has begun transforming its acquisition process to create more efficient and effective ways to acquire goods and services faster, better, and cheaper (DAU, 2005). The exponential rate of technological advance combined with the availability of new technologies on the commercial market has added a sense of urgency to the acquisition environment. The DoD would like to access these advances before adversaries can use them against the US.

A good example of the types of changes sought is the pursuit of evolutionary acquisition strategies that rely on spiral development processes. This approach focuses on providing the warfighter with an initial capability (that may not be the final capability) as a tradeoff for earlier delivery, flexibility, affordability, and risk reduction. The capabilities delivered are provided over a shorter period of time, followed by subsequent increments of capability over time that incorporate the latest technology and flexibility to reach the full capability of the system (Apte, 2005).

In a Defense Science Board (DSB) summer study on transformation (DSB, 2006), it was recommended that the Undersecretary of Defense Acquisition, Technology & Logistics (AT&L)

> should renew efforts to remove barriers that prevent the entry of non-tra-
> ditional companies to the Defense business and Defense access to com-
> mercial technology, attacking the myriad rules, regulations, and practices
> that limit the use of OTA, Part 12, and other programs to reach beyond
> traditional defense companies.

The study goes on to recommend intense integration with global and commercial supply chains, as well as transforming the export license process.

Summary

Where are defense expenditures headed? *The Economist* (2023) reports,

> We estimate that total new defense commitments and forecast spending
> increases, if implemented, will generate over $200 billion in extra defense

spending globally each year. It could be a lot more. Imagine that countries which currently spend less than 2% of GDP per year meet that level and that the remainder increase spending by half a percentage point of GDP. Global defense outlays would rise by close to $700bn a year.

RESPONSES TO EXPLOITATION

An integrated response to mitigate exploitation is more likely to be enacted rather than piecemeal pieces of legislation having to overcome separate battles. Hence, I propose the following mitigation agenda.

Mitigation Agenda

Legislation will be needed to address how to provide responses to exploitations of health and safety. Who is responsible for the consequences of societal exploitation and how do they compensate society? Taxation to address externalities would be warranted. These taxes would be paid upon purchase of a vehicle and for the annual use of the vehicle.

Roughly 20 million vehicles are purchased annually in the US and there are 300 million vehicles on the road. Assuming a purchase tax of $5,000 and an annual tax of $1,000, revenue would equal $100 billion for purchases and $300 billion for annual use. A total of $400 billion could be deposited annually in the Environmental Trust Fund, the use of which would be limited to remediating the consequences of exploitation.

Of course, remediating the consequences of CO_2 emissions and pollution will become increasingly costly if we do not manage these challenges rather than just respond to their occurrence. To this end, we need legislation that mandates the development and operation of failure management capabilities (Porter, 2020; Rouse, 2021). The necessary decision support capabilities have been conceptualized. They need to be deployed at scale.

Legislation to address fraud, waste, and abuse needs to reflect an understanding of the causes of waste, fraud, and abuse. This is due in part to the lack of competitive market forces, as well as the nature of cost plus contracts and effective monopolies. These causes are aggravated by political needs to sustain jobs despite the capabilities being produced and operated no longer providing value.

Legislation is needed to reestablish competition in defense procurements. For example, there should be at least two providers of F-35 aircraft. Lockheed Martin, in this case, would fiercely object. However, the government is the sole customer and has enormous leverage to force companies to agree to return to the competitive market models of the past.

Acquisition reform to streamline defense acquisition needs to be mandated. We do not need another Packard Commission. Several recent studies, e.g., DoD (2018), have provided almost 100 detailed recommendations for the changes needed. Legislation is needed to enact recommended improvements and repeal hindrances.

Finally, legislation is needed to provide laws and regulations to address prosecution of more egregious instances of waste, fraud, and abuse. Defense contractors should not be shielded from such legal actions. The Inspector General should be proactive in such pursuits.

Role of Government

The charters of the government agencies involved in the mitigation agenda are summarized in Table 3.3. A few agencies not discussed above are included due to their particular relevance to environment and safety. Environment risks and disasters are concerns of EPA, Federal Emergency Management Agency (FEMA), and National Oceanic and Atmospheric Administration (NOAA). Vehicle and work safety are addressed by Federal Aviation Administration (FAA), Federal Railroad Administration (FRA), International Civil Aviation Organization (ICAO), National Institute for Occupational Safety and Health (NIOSH), National Highway Traffic Safety Administration (NHTSA), and Occupational Safety and Health Administration (OSHA).

CONCLUSIONS

Transportation, and mobility in general, are central to the movement of people and goods that are essential for the economic health of our society. There have been centuries of innovations. In the twentieth century, the

TABLE 3.3

Selected US Government Agencies

Agency (Founding)	Agency Charter
EPA (1970)	The Environmental Protection Agency is an independent executive agency of the United States federal government tasked with environmental protection matters.
FAA (1958)	The Federal Aviation Administration is the largest transportation agency of the US government and regulates all aspects of civil aviation in the country as well as over surrounding international waters.
FEMA (1979)	The Federal Emergency Management Agency is an agency of the United States Department of Homeland Security whose mission is helping people before, during, and after disasters.
FRA (1967)	The Federal Railroad Administration is an agency in the United States Department of Transportation enabling the safe, reliable, and efficient movement of people and goods.
ICAO (1944)	The International Civil Aviation Organization is a specialized agency of the United Nations that coordinates the principles and techniques of international air navigation and fosters the planning and development of international air transport to ensure safe and orderly growth.
NIOSH (1970)	The National Institute for Occupational Safety and Health is the United States federal agency responsible for conducting research and making recommendations for the prevention of work-related injury and illness.
NHTSA (1970)	The National Highway Traffic Safety Administration is an agency of the US federal government, part of the Department of Transportation. It describes its mission as "Save lives, prevent injuries, reduce vehicle-related crashes" related to transportation safety in the United States.
NOAA (1970)	The National Oceanic and Atmospheric Administration is a Washington, DC-based scientific and regulatory agency within the United States Department of Commerce.
OSHA (1971)	The Occupational Safety and Health Administration is a large regulatory agency of the United States Department of Labor that originally had federal visitorial powers to inspect and examine workplaces, whose workplace safety inspections have been shown to reduce injury rates and injury costs without adverse effects on employment, sales, credit ratings, or firm survival.

first powered flight of the Wright brothers was in 1903 and the Apollo astronauts landed on the moon in 1969, amazing feats happening within one human lifetime.

Transportation benefits society, but it also exploits the environment in a variety of ways, ranging from CO_2 emissions and pollution to traffic congestion and accidents. A human-centered society aspires to balance human well-being. Aggressive exploitation is incompatible with this objective. However, exploitation is a natural tendency among people focused solely on their own goals. Consequently, we need to understand the hallmarks of exploitation and have mechanisms that can mitigate such tendencies.

REFERENCES

APA. (2014). Road rage: What makes some people more prone to anger behind the wheel. *American Psychological Association.* https://www.apa.org/topics/anger/road-rage.

Apte, A. (2005). *Spiral Development: A Perspective.* Monterey, CA: Naval Postgraduate School, Graduate School of Business and Public Policy.

Augustine, N.R. (1984). *Augustine's Laws.* Reston, VA: American Institute of Aeronautics & Astronautics.

Baker, P.C. (2023). It's easy to see what's wrong with car culture: Fixing it is harder. *Washington Post,* May 28.

Boot, M. (2023). An Army command like no other seeks to master the future of war. *Washington Post,* May 28, 2023

Bright, C.D. (1978). *The Jet Makers: The Aerospace Industry from 1945 to 1972.* Lawrence, KS: University Press of Kansas.

BTS. (2023). *Transportation Services Contributed 5.6% to U.S. GDP in 2021: An Increase from 5.4% in 2020 but Below 5.8% in 2019.* Washington, DC: Bureau of Transportation Statistics.

Cancian, M. (1995). Acquisition reform: It's not as easy as it seems. *Acquisition Review Quarterly* (Summer),(3) 190–192.

Casti, J. (1989). *Paradigms Lost: Images of Man in the Mirror of Science.* New York: Morrow.

CBS. (2023). Weapons contractors hitting department of defense with inflated prices for planes, submarines, missiles. *60 Minutes.* https://www.cbsnews.com/amp/news/weapons-contractors-price-gouging-pentagon-60-minutes-transcript-2023-05-21/.

CDC. (2022). *Global Road Safety.* Atlanta, GA: Centers for Disease Prevention and Control.

CDC. (2023). *Impaired Driving: Get the Facts.* Atlanta, GA: Centers for Disease Prevention and Control.

Chandler, A.D. Jr. (Ed.). (1965). *The Railroads: The Nation's First Big Business.* New York: Harcourt, Brace, & World.

Christensen, D.S., Searle, D.A., & Vickery, C. (1999). The impact of the Packard Commission's recommendations on reducing cost overruns on defense acquisition contracts. *Acquisition Review Quarterly* (Summer), 252–256.

DAU. (2005). *Introduction to Defense Acquisition Management* (7th Edition). Washington, DC: Department of Defense, Defense Acquisition University Press.

DePillis, L., & Smialek, J. (2023). Why is inflation so stubborn? Cars are part of the answer. *New York Times,* May 20.

DoD. (2018). *Advisory Panel on Streamlining and Codifying Acquisition Regulations: Section 809 Report*. Washington, DC: US Department of Defense.

DOT. (2023). *Transportation Employment*. Washington, DC: US Department of Transportation.

Drezner, J.A., Jarvaise, J., Hess, R., Hough, P., & Norton, D. (1993). *An Analysis of Weapon System Cost Growth* (MR-291-AF). Santa Monica, CA: RAND Corporation.

DSB. (2006). *Transformation: A Progress Assessment* (Vol. 1). Washington, DC: Defense Science Board.

Dunbaugh, E.L. (1992). *Night Boat to New England: 1815–1900*. New York: Greenwood Press.

Economist. (2023a). Autonomous vehicles are coming, but slowly: The next challenge for legacy firms in to adapt to autonomy. *The Economist*, April 14.

Economist. (2023b). The cost of the global arms race. *The Economist*, May 23.

EPA. (2023). *Inventory of U.S. Greenhouse Gas Emissions and Sinks*. Washington, DC: Environmental Protection Agency.

Fuller, R., Landrigan, P.J., Balakrishnan, K., Bathan, G., Bose-O'Reilly, S., & Brauer, M. et al. (2022). Pollution and health: A progress update. *The Lancet: Planetary Health*, 6 (6), 535–547.

Heppenheimer, T.A. (1993). The jet plane is born. *Invention & Technology* (Fall), 44–56.

Heppenheimer, T.A. (1994). The dream of the flying wing. *Invention & Technology* (Winter), 55–63.

Hilton, G.W. (1993). The wrong track. *Invention & Technology* (Spring), 46–54.

Jensen, O. (1975). *Railroads in America*. New York: American Heritage.

Knowles, D. (2023). *Carmageddon: How Cars Make Life Worse and What to Do About It*. New York: Harry N. Abrams.

Laczkowski, K., Okeke-Agba, A., Voelker, A., & Weddle, B. (2023). *Full Speed Ahead: The Automotive Sector's Resilience Imperative*. New York: McKinsey & Company.

Levine, P. (2020). *Defense Management Reform: How to Make the Pentagon Work Better and Cost Less*. Palo Alto, CA: Stanford University Press.

Lipton, E. (2023). The Pentagon saw a warship boondoggle: Congress saw jobs. *New York Times*, February 4.

Magaziner, I., & Patinkin, M. (1989). *The Silent War: Inside the Global Business Battles Shaping America's Future*. New York: Random House.

McCullough, D. (2016).*The Wright Brothers*. New York: Simon & Schuster.

Meyersohn, N. (2023). This little-known rule shapes parking in America: Cities are reversing it. *CNN*. https://www.cnn.com/2023/05/20/business/parking-minimums -cars-transportation-urban-planning/index.html.

Mintz, J. (1997). How a dinner led to a feeding frenzy. *Washington Post*, July 4.

Moore, G.A. (1991). *Crossing the Chasm: Marketing and Selling Technology Products to Mainstream Customers*. New York: Harper Business.

Negroni, C. (2023). Deadly traffic in suburbia points to deep-seated structural problems. *New York Times*, May 20.

Packard, D. (1986). *A Quest for Excellence: Final Report to the President by the President's Blue Ribbon Commission on Defense Management*. Washington, DC: The Commission.

Pennock, M.J., Rouse, W.B., & Kollar, D.L. (2007). Transforming the acquisition enter-prise: A framework for analysis and a case study of ship acquisition. *Journal of Systems Engineering*, 10 (2), 99–117.

Porter, D.L. (2020). *Flight Failure: Investigating the Nuts and Bolts of Air Disasters and Aviation Safety.* New York: Prometheus.

Rae, J.B. (1968). *Climb to Greatness: The American Aircraft Industry, 1920–1960.* Cambridge, MA: MIT Press.

Rouse, W.B. (1996) *Start Where You Are: Matching Your Strategy to Your Marketplace.* San Francisco, CA: Jossey-Bass.

Rouse, W.B. (2021). *Failure Management: Malfunctions of Technologies, Organizations and Society.* Oxford: Oxford University Press.

Shulman, K. (2023). MIT Mobility Initiative thinks forward: Platform merges public, private, and academic spheres to help shape the future of transportation. *Spectrum* (Spring).

Werbach, A. (2013). The American commuter spends 38 hours a year stuck in traffic. *The Atlantic,* February 6.

White, N. (1993). From tractor to tank. *Invention & Technology* (Fall), 58–63.

Wohleber, C. (1993). Straight up. *Invention & Technology* (Winter), 26–38.

Womack, J.P., Jones, D.T., & Roos, D. (1991). *The Machine That Changed the World: The Story of Lean Production.* New York: Harper.

Wright, S. (2023). Everything about carmaking is changing at once. *The Economist,* April 14.

4

Computers and Communications

Innovations in transportation, and related technologies, as outlined in Chapter 3 drove economic growth in the US for quite some time. However, the dominance of this ecosystem was displaced by the mid-twentieth century by computers and communications. The seeds of this transformation have a rich history (Isaacson, 2014), including Franklin and electricity in 1752 (Isaacson, 2003), Bell and the telephone in 1876 (Grosvenor & Wesson, 2016), and Edison and electric lighting in 1880 (Jonnes, 2003). However, the market innovations in computers and communications emerged in the 1940s.

INNOVATION IN COMPUTING AND COMMUNICATIONS

The evolution of computer technology and the computer industry took hundreds of years. It is important to differentiate the evolution of computing technology from that of the computer industry. Computing technology is very old, dating from the abacus thousands of years ago. People have wanted to add and subtract numbers for a long, long time (Isaacson, 2014).

The first mechanical adding machine was built more than 300 years ago by Frenchman Blaise Pascal. German Gottfried Wilhelm Leibniz, after seeing Pascal's machine, created the Stepped Reckoner in 1673. This device could also multiply, divide, and perform square roots. The first commercially available calculator was Thomas de Colmar's arithmometer in 1820.

DOI: 10.4324/9781003462361-4

Charles Babbage conceived the first digital computer in the 1830s. He envisioned this computer – the Analytical Engine – as powered by steam. (Recall from Chapter 3 that steam power was "high tech" in the 1830s.) Babbage's vision was never realized due to a lack of precision techniques for fabricating parts.

Babbage got his idea for a digital computer from Frenchman Joseph-Marie Jacquard's punch-card-programmed looms, developed in the early 1800s. He was also aware of the work of Englishman George Boole who performed pioneering research in binary logic in the mid-1800s. Binary logic later became the key to electronic computing.

Jacquard's punched card method for controlling looms also influenced American Herman Hollerith who invented a card-based system for tabulating the results of the 1890 census. Hollerith's venture led to what would later become IBM, under the leadership of Thomas J. Watson Sr. In *Father, Son, and Co.* (1990), Thomas J. Watson Jr. not surprisingly asserts that "In the history of industrialization, punch-card machines belong right up there with the Jacquard loom, the cotton gin, and the locomotive." The adoption of punched cards for computing constitutes a good example of a crossover situation.

Having mentioned IBM, it is important that I now shift the emphasis from computing technology to the computing industry. The many stories underlying the evolution of this industry provide a rich array of insights into how enterprises deal with change. Many of these stories start in the mid-1800s.

Roots of the Industry

James W. Cortada in *Before the Computer* (1993) chronicles the emergence of the computer industry in the period 1865–1956. During this period, IBM, NCR, Burroughs, Remington Rand, and other companies became dominant in the business equipment industry with tabulators (IBM), cash registers (NCR), calculators (Burroughs), and typewriters (Remington). The dominance of these companies set the stage for their becoming primary players in the computer market.

Cortada notes that many mechanical aids were available for computing and managing data long before computers became available. William S. Burroughs saw the market need for adding machines. James Ritty, and subsequently John H. Patterson, envisioned the potential demand for cash registers. Christopher L. Sholes identified the potential for typewriters. As noted earlier, Herman Hollerith invented a tabulator for compiling the results of the US census. Prior to 1920, these business machines were all independently sold with any particular company offering only one type of machine. Subsequently, most of these types of machines were marketed by the same companies.

It is interesting to consider why there was demand for these business machines. Cortada argues that starting in the 1840s, the American economy went through a long period – more than 100 years – of continual expansion and industrialization. Despite the Civil War in the 1860s, the financial panic in the 1870s, and a severe depression in the 1890s, the economic expansion continued with major new ventures in railroads, steel mills, and chemical plants. This not only required substantial investments in technology. Investments in marketing and distribution channels, as well as the development of management systems, were also central to success. These latter investments provided the impetus for the development of the types of business machines outlined in the following paragraphs.

As noted earlier, the history of adding machines and calculators dates back hundreds of years to mathematicians – for example, Pascal and Leibniz – and others who sought aids to calculation. After several years of work, William Burroughs patented an adding machine in 1885, the same year that he formed the Arithmometer Company. Burroughs was not the only one to sense the potential market for calculators. For example, Dorr E. Felt invented one of the first key-operated calculating machines and the firm of Felt and Tarrant was formed in 1886.

By 1895, following 15 years of work by Burroughs, the calculator market started to blossom. By the year of Burrough's death – 1898 – his company's products had achieved some market acceptance. The Burroughs Adding and Listing Machine was quite popular by the early 1900s. In recognition of his contributions, the company was reincorporated in 1904 as the Burroughs Adding Machine Company. Thus, almost 25 years after he started and eight years after his death, Burroughs was an unqualified success. This is yet another example of both vision quest and evolution situations.

However, this slowly emerging victory was not complete and, in retrospect, was temporary. There was a crowded field of competitors in the calculator business. Frequently emerging technological improvements had to be matched or even established vendors could be superseded by other, usually new, firms. Typically, these firms had a single product or technology to sell. If we change the word "calculator" to "software," the description in this paragraph would be as relevant today as it was more than 100 years ago.

The cash register was invented by James Ritty in the late 1870s in Dayton, Ohio. A few years later, Ritty sold the business to Jacob Eckert who renamed the company the National Manufacturing Company. John Patterson bought controlling interest in 1884 and changed the company's name to National Cash Register Company. By 1888, Patterson had a payroll of 80.

Patterson is remembered as the entrepreneur who made salesmanship into a science – his disciples included Thomas J. Watson Sr. Patterson thoroughly trained his salespeople and continually refined the marketing and sales approach that enabled selling cash registers. Nevertheless, by 1895, there were 84 companies selling, or attempting to sell, cash registers. This period constituted the early stages of a consolidation situation within the cash register industry.

The typewriter emerged during the same period of time although, as with the other business machines, early developments dated back over 150 years. Christopher Sholes developed the typewriter to the point of being marketable. He obtained financial backing from James Densmore, who founded an established manufacturing company, Remington, to manufacture Sholes' typewriter.

Remington had significant difficulties gaining momentum. These problems were due to marketing problems, as is often the case for start-ups. Further, competitors emerged quickly in the typewriter market. Remington was also slow to respond to technological change which affected sales. These types of problems and others were to continue to plague Remington throughout the emergence of the computer industry and, as later discussed, led to their loss of a decisive lead in the computer industry in the 1950s.

By the early 1900s, there were four large typewriter companies including the former Remington – now called the Union Typewriter Company – Underwood, L.C. Smith, and Royal. At this point, the industry exhibited elements of a crossing-the-chasm situation, as well as early elements of the consolidation situation. Thus, the problems that the computer hardware industry faced in the late 1980s and early 1990s, as well as the problems likely to emerge in the computer software industry, are by no means new to many of the players in the business machines industry.

As discussed earlier, Herman Hollerith invented the tabulator. Hollerith developed the concept while he was a clerk at the Census Bureau. Cortada notes that Hollerith's idea was due, in part, to comments by John S. Billings, director of the Division of Vital Statistics, that "there ought to be some mechanical way of doing this job, something on the principle of the Jacquard loom."

Hollerith was at the center of the resulting tabulating technology for many years. He single-handedly formed the Tabulating Machine Company in 1889 and his tabulating equipment was used for the census of 1890. Hollerith joined others to form the Computing-Tabulating-Recording Company (C-T-R) in 1911 because he needed an infusion of capital to continue expanding. Thomas J. Watson Sr., a former NCR executive, was hired in 1914 as general manager. The company changed its name to IBM in 1924.

One of Hollerith's contributions was his pioneering the practice of renting data processing equipment. Under Watson's tutelage, the constant introduction of new products led to continual success. These product innovations were, for the most part, due to customers' demands and careful monitoring of competitors' offerings.

The Census Bureau decided that they needed more than a single source of tabulating equipment. To this end, they encouraged James Powers, an employee, to create competing equipment. Powers left the Census Bureau in 1911 to form the Powers Accounting Machine Company. The US government gave Powers the right to patent the devices that he had developed on behalf of the government. Powers merged with Remington-Rand in 1927

Initial products from Powers were functionally superior to Hollerith's, a situation often encountered by IBM. However, Watson's skill in marketing and customer relations came to overshadow Power's engineering abilities. IBM's consummate skill became one of assuring customers that their data processing problems would be solved, rather than emphasizing the innovativeness of their technologies. While IBM had to respond when new technologies emerged – as I later discuss – they kept their focus on supporting customers. Consequently, customers grew to increasingly depend on them. Nevertheless, Powers/ Remington-Rand remained important players and, as World War II approached, sales of tabulating machines were dominated by IBM and Remington-Rand.

Cortada concludes that tabulating machines were the forerunners of computers. Unlike the cash register, calculator, and typewriter, tabulators were designed to handle large amounts of data. Eventually, in the 1930s and 1940s, calculators and tabulators merged as businesses needed to process ever-increasing amounts of data. Much more recently, cash registers and typewriters have, in effect, become computers. Thus, these four industries eventually converged.

Some of the reasons for this convergence were technical in nature. For example, keyboards became a common element of all of these types of business machines. Related technologies that may have facilitated convergence were the telegraph and telephone.

Of course, a primary motivating factor in the search for synergies was the commonality of customers across these machines. This factor was probably a strong influence in the merging of firms to provide a wider variety of products via more highly integrated companies. Cortada indicates that, by 1924–25, there were 26 vendors of adding machines, 14 of calculating machines, 8 of bookkeeping machines, and 6 of billing machines. However, between World War I and the end of the 1920s, many consolidations occurred. This was prompted in part by the increasingly capital-intensive nature of the competition.

We can see a consolidation situation emerging here across industry segments. Initially, consolidation occurred within each segment of the business machine industry – for example, by adding machines or typewriters. However, in more recent years, the distinctions among these types of machines have slowly but surely disappeared. Thus, we now see most people doing their "typewriting" on personal computers rather than typewriters. Consolidations, therefore, need not stay within one stream of development.

Cortada's discussions of the maturation of these technologies can easily be cast as evolution situations. All of these types of business machines met with little enthusiasm when they were first developed. It then took many years before the methods and costs of production and marketing were sufficiently understood and controllable to be able to provide sufficient value to the marketplace at reasonable prices. It was also important to be able to demonstrate convincingly that a sufficient range of applications could benefit from the use of these machines. These lessons are as true today as they were then, earlier in this century, as well as much earlier for steamboats.

He notes that government and large industrial enterprises were the first customers. They could afford to use new technologies earlier than smaller enterprises. As the use of these machines spread, customers became more knowledgeable and their demands for additional functionality increased. In addition, service and education were seen as essential if customers were to allow themselves to become increasingly dependent upon these machines. Meeting the demands for greater functionality and reliability, as well as increasingly supportive service, required that competitors invest more to stay in the business. Many companies' inability to sustain such investments was one of the factors promoting consolidation.

Cortada reflects on the impact on the industry of people such as Burroughs and Watson. While he grants that they provided important leadership, he suggests that eventual success was more due to a wide range of organizations and people who sought to find the means for dealing with the explosion of business information that accompanied the continual economic expansion and industrialization. More specifically, people like Burroughs and Watson were at the right place at the right time but, according to Cortada, did not create the times.

Here we see an interesting contrast between organic and synthetic views. The pioneers in the business machine industry certainly demonstrated their abilities to synthesize solutions to increasingly important business problems. However, this process was driven by the recognition of organic forces and trends. Further, the processes whereby they marketed, sold, and supported these machines very much reflected the organic nature of the marketplace.

Early Digital Computing

The emergence of digital computing and the process of maturation of the computer industry have been described by Franklin M. Fisher, James W. McKie, and Richard B. Mancke in *IBM and the U.S. Data Processing Industry* (1983). A somewhat different perspective is provided by Norman Macrae in his biography *John von Neumann* (1992).

Macrae asserts that digital computers and electronic computing emerged because of 20 years of purely academic research in quantum theory, which ushered in the electronics age. He also gives much credit to J. Presper Eckert at the University of Pennsylvania and "one of the cleverest men in the world" – John von Neumann of Princeton.

The key sequence of events starts with John V. Atansoff of Iowa State who built a prototype of an electromechanical digital computer in 1939. Other electromechanical computers include the IBM-sponsored Automatic Sequence Controlled Calculator (also known as the Mark I) developed in 1944 at Harvard by Howard Aiken, and a computer developed by Bell Laboratories during the same period.

John W. Mauchly joined the University of Pennsylvania faculty in 1942, soon after having met John Atanasoff who by now was working on a vacuum tube-based computer concept. J. Presper Eckert, a young engineer at U. Penn, was immediately taken with Mauchly's articulation of the idea. Work started in 1943 with support from the Army's Ballistics Research Laboratory. The Army was interested in faster ways to create firing tables for artillery use.

By 1946, they had completed the Electronic Numerical Integrator and Calculator, ENIAC, which was the first all-purpose, all-electronic digital computer. Avoiding the electrically driven mechanical relays of the earlier computers resulted in a speed up of a factor of 1000. However, ENIAC, and later EDVAC (Electronic Discrete Variable Computer) in 1950, were by no means immediately successful. Businesses, in particular IBM, dismissed the concept as too expensive and too risky.

Nevertheless, Von Neumann, according to Macrae, saw the potential immediately and his thinking quickly outpaced Eckert and Mauchly. Von Neumann realized that the essence of computing was the logical functions performed and that stored-program computing was the necessary next step. He outlined this next step in what became known as the First Draft which Macrae asserts "served as a model for virtually all future studies of logical design of computers." Working at the Institute for Advanced Study (IAS) at Princeton, Von Neumann and his team continued their work on computer architectures.

By 1952, there were seven descendants of the IAS computer including MANIAC (Los Alamos), JOHNNIAC (Rand Corporation), AVIDAC (Argonne National Laboratory), ORDVAC (Aberdeen Proving Ground), ORACLE (Oak Ridge National Laboratory), ILLIAC (University of Illinois), and most important the IBM 701 which led IBM into world dominance.

Eckert and Mauchly were not waiting in the wings during this period. They left the University of Pennsylvania in 1946 to set up the Eckert-Mauchly Corporation. They built BINAC (Binary Automatic Computer) for Northrop Corporation in 1950, and UNIVAC (Universal Automatic Computer) for the Census Bureau in 1951.

Eckert and Mauchly approached IBM for investment capital during this period. However, IBM feared anti-trust problems and declined. Subsequently, they were bought in 1950–51 by Remington-Rand. In 1955, Remington-Rand was bought by Sperry, creating Sperry Rand. Thus, we see continuing consolidation.

The effects of the intellectual relationship between Eckert-Mauchly and John von Neumann had long-lasting effects. Sperry Rand brought litigation against other computer companies, claiming that they had appropriated Eckert and Mauchly ideas. These claims were dismissed in 1973 based on a judgment that these ideas were in the public domain due to the nature of von Neumann's First Draft. Another factor in the dismissal was the fact that the original idea was Atanasoff's.

This vignette serves to highlight the fact that starting in the early to mid-1950s, the race to gain market share in the growing computer industry became increasingly heated. Remington-Rand was the first out of the starting blocks. As noted earlier, they entered the computer business by acquiring Eckert-Mauchly in 1950. In 1952, they acquired Engineering Research Associates which was formed in 1946 by William Norris and others.

Cortada concludes that consolidations such as those initiated by Remington-Rand were due to low-profit margins in an increasingly competitive industry. He notes that such consolidations first became a recognizable pattern with typewriter manufacturers and then with adding and tabulating machine vendors. These consolidations could result in economies of scale if marketing and manufacturing were integrated.

The patterns recognized by Cortada can be generalized to capture many, and probably most, of the consolidation situations discussed thus far. Such stories start with technologies – usually after experiencing long evolution situations – becoming sufficiently mature to penetrate broader markets. This maturity involves not just the product technology, but also the technology necessary for manufacturing, support, marketing, and sales. When all these pieces are in place, crossing-the-chasm situations emerge.

Initial success in broader markets leads, often fairly quickly, to dramatic increases in the number of players. Each of these players scrambles for market share, which may be relatively easy during initial steady growth situations. Eventually, however, market share only comes with lower prices and/or higher costs, e.g., increased costs of selling. This leads to lower gross and net profit margins. The subsequent need for capital to compete leads, apparently inevitably, to consolidation situations.

Fisher and colleagues point out in the case of Remington-Rand that the benefits of consolidation are far from automatic. They quote William Norris, "Remington-Rand faltered at the crucial time when it had a chance to take over the computer market. The hesitation was the result of Jim Rand being too old to be able to carry through on a great opportunity." Norris also said that Sperry Rand's failure to focus on the computer business was one of the reasons that he left to form Control Data Corporation (CDC) in 1957. Fisher and colleagues quote *Business Week*'s observation that Sperry "snatched defeat from the jaws of victory."

Remington-Rand had some early success including selling UNIVAC machines to the Census Bureau, which displaced IBM tabulators. Thus, IBM certainly took notice. However, as Thomas Watson Jr. notes, IBM eventually beat out Remington-Rand because Rand was more of a conglomerate than a computer company. They did not put their money and hearts behind the technology.

Fisher observes that Rand had no computer-related profit centers until 1964. In other words, they treated computers just like any other piece of equipment or office furniture. IBM, in contrast, recognized the tremendous potential of computers and how they had to be marketed.

Thomas Watson Jr. asserts that IBM succeeded by focusing on deep system knowledge which helped their customers succeed. Reflecting on IBM's success in overcoming Remington-Rand's head start, Cortada concludes "all available evidence points to the effectiveness of having a corporate strategy that works as opposed to simply allowing market conditions to control business rhythms opportunistically." He elaborates on this, noting "abhorrence of reacting as opposed to responding proactively remained one of the fundamental characteristics of IBM's culture deep into the twentieth century."

The above observations are central. Fairly quickly (although not immediately – see below), IBM recognized what was likely to happen in the business machines industry. They responded with a strategy that enabled them to have some degree of control. More specifically, IBM organically responded to long-term market trends by synthetically developing a customer-oriented strategy that helped their customers deal successfully with trends that were affecting them.

This balancing of the organic and synthetic often is a central aspect of success, especially when you are involved in a consolidation situation. In contrast, in vision quest and evolution situations, such balancing tends to be less central because companies in such situations usually do not have to deal with an increasing abundance of competitors. However, once they transition to a crossing-the-chasm situation, and especially if they eventually become involved in a consolidation situation, they may need balancing skills whose development is likely to have been overlooked.

Despite the story I have just outlined, Remington-Rand remained a prime competitor for quite some time. During the 1950s, both IBM and Remington-Rand prospered, as did Burroughs, NCR, and Underwood. This was due to the increasing desire of large organizations to process large amounts of data in order to manage their enterprises better, as well as a relatively strong economy that enabled investments in data processing equipment. Cortada notes that government funding of post-war R&D also played a very significant role. The result was that by 1954 there were 23 firms in the computer business, not counting the aircraft companies and the universities.

Fisher and colleagues chronicle the emergence and consolidation of a variety of players in the computer industry during the 1950s and 1960s. In 1953, NCR acquired Computer Research Corporation from Northrop Aviation. In 1956, Burroughs acquired Electrodata. In 1957, Honeywell bought Raytheon's share of Datamatic Corporation which they had formed in 1955. In 1961, Philco departed from the computer business, in part because it was acquired by Ford. In 1963, CDC made seven acquisitions, including Bendix's computer operations. In 1969, GE sold its computer business to Honeywell, based on their own assessment that their product lines were obsolete and their technical position was lagging. In 1971, Sperry Rand bought RCA's computer business, which had been in trouble for quite some time.

These consolidation situations reflect missed opportunities due to outright product failures, the inability of some companies to transform themselves from electromechanical cultures to electronics, and often failures to focus on being in the computer business. By the early 1960s, IBM dominated the industry with almost ten times the computer-related revenues of the number two competitor, Sperry Rand, followed by AT&T, CDC, Philco, Burroughs, GE, NCR, Honeywell, and RCA. Just a few years later, the rank ordering was IBM, Sperry Rand, Honeywell, Burroughs, NCR, CDC, and SDS (Scientific Data Systems).

There was much more consolidation to come, as well as several new, strong competitors. However, rather than simply list these events, I want to pursue these stories – the stories of IBM, DEC, and Apple – in more depth. In this way, we gain much deeper insights into the dominant situations that have been experienced by the computer industry.

In particular, we gain insight into four epochs of the computer industry. The first epoch emphasized centralized computing via large mainframe computers. The second epoch focused on interactive computing using much smaller minicomputers. The third epoch, personal computing, was based on microcomputers. The fourth epoch, digital devices, sets the stage for the next chapter.

Centralized Computing – IBM

The history of International Business Machines (IBM) has been well documented by many commentators, several of whom I have cited earlier. Important additional sources are Thomas J. Watson, Jr's *Father, Son, & Co.* (1990) and Kevin Maney's *The Maverick and His Machine: Thomas H. Watson Sr. and the Making of IBM* (2003) which provide more personal perspectives. In this section, I describe several developments in the computer industry from an IBM-centered point of view.

As is not surprising, the history of IBM for the Watsons begins with Thomas Watson Sr. becoming general manager of the Computing-Tabulating-Recording Company (C-T-R) in 1914. Watson had learned the concepts, principles, methods, and tools of professional, customer-oriented salesmanship from the almost legendary John Patterson of NCR. Watson further refined this philosophy and approach which became the hallmark of the company that was to become IBM in 1924.

For the initial decades of the Watson leadership – which included Watson Sr. and later Watson Jr. – IBM was in the tabulator business as described earlier in this section. This business grew dramatically. During World War II, the company tripled in size due to military contracts.

Anticipating the inevitable drop in military orders immediately following the war, the Watsons aggressively added sales capacity. This enabled IBM to take advantage of the post-war boom in demand for goods and services not available during the war. As retailers and wholesalers rapidly expanded their businesses, these companies' needs for data processing also expanded and IBM was well-positioned to prosper.

Watson Jr. tells an interesting story of how IBM got into the electronics business. Tabulators had, until that time, been electromechanical devices. IBM had been developing and evaluating a vacuum tube-based multiplier in its R&D labs. This electronic multiplier was integrated into one of IBM's tabulators. However, due to the overall slowness of the mechanical systems in this tabulator, the electronic multiplier provided no overall speed advantage. Thus, this hybrid tabulator would provide customers with no additional value added.

The younger Watson argued that they should put the product on the market, despite this lack of additional benefits. While they might not sell any of these systems, they would be able to claim that they had the world's first electronic tabulating system. The public relations value of being able to make this claim would justify writing off the investment made in a system that provided no value added. The result was the IBM 603. In spite of everyone's expectations, this gimmick became a market success and IBM was launched in the electronics business.

In the 1940s, IBM had been funding research at the University of Pennsylvania and Harvard University. As I described earlier, significant developments in digital computing occurred during this period. However, the Watsons saw no market potential for computers, except perhaps in the scientific area. Watson Sr. saw punch-card machines and computers as relevant to two completely different realms – business and science/engineering, respectively.

This is not as surprising as it may sound. As far back as Pascal and Leibniz, developments in computation were driven by the desire to perform calculations involving engineering and scientific formulae. Many of the developments in the 1940s – such as those of Eckert and Mauchly at the University of Pennsylvania – were funded for the purpose of computing ballistic trajectories rather than payrolls and financial statements. However, the Watsons and many others were experiencing a crossover situation whereby computing's biggest impact would soon be in business.

As I noted earlier, Eckert and Mauchly left the University of Pennsylvania to bring the UNIVAC to the market. By the early 1950s, Remington-Rand had placed UNIVAC machines at the Census Bureau which, as I have already indicated, displaced IBM's tabulators. This was one of many competitive challenges that propelled IBM into the computer business.

In another instance, IBM learned that Remington-Rand planned to employ magnetic tape rather than punch cards as a primary media. In response, IBM engineers came up with a magnetic tape-based solution. However, Watson Sr. rejected the use of magnetic tape.

Watson Jr. was concerned about the wisdom of this decision. He asked his top salesmen if magnetic tape was the future – they all said "no." He reflected,

> I was beginning to learn that the majority, even the majority of top performers, are never the ones to ask when you need to make a move. You've got to feel what's going on in the world and then make the move yourself. It's purely visceral.

(Watson, 1990)

We can see an interesting contrast in the reactions of the two Watsons. The older Watson was determined to stay with the old paradigm, one to which he had very substantially contributed. The IBM culture supported him in this decision. However, sticking with the punch card paradigm would have seriously impeded the company. The younger Watson, in contrast, was not as invested in the old paradigm and facilitated change in the right direction.

Thus, we see a new aspect of the vision quest. The keeper of the vision can lead the enterprise forward, but they can also hold the enterprise back. This problem stems from people becoming trapped by their predominant metaphors. In this example, they became entrapped by the idea that they were selling card-processing equipment rather than information processing equipment.

This is a good example of a paradigm lost situation. The vision quest – with surprisingly low probability – eventually leads to substantial success. However, the visionary paradigm seldom continues to be the most compelling vision. Unfortunately, the original visionary may be one of the last to recognize when his or her paradigm has been lost to new visions.

This tendency is quite natural and common. It can be avoided – or its effects can be substantially lessened – by focusing on problems rather than solutions. Being problem-centered means that you emphasize understanding the benefits that customers need and want rather than the particular technologies in which these benefits are embodied. These needs and wants are likely to persist much longer than any particular technology.

A primary factor in IBM's catching up and eventually moving ahead of Remington-Rand was their involvement in the SAGE project at MIT's Lincoln Laboratory. The SAGE concept grew out of work during the late 1940s on Project Whirlwind. This project involved computer-based simulation and was led by Jay Forrester. The Air Force decided to employ this technology to develop SAGE (Semi-Automated Ground Environment) for its air defense needs. IBM was selected as the contractor to work with MIT during this development effort.

Until the late 1950s, SAGE computers accounted for almost half of IBM's computer sales. Thus, we see both the technology and market acceptance fitting into a story of evolution rather than revolution. We also see computers being used for technical rather than business applications. The immense business data processing market did not, by any means, immediately embrace computers.

As discussed earlier, a key in IBM's eventual dominance was its commitment to becoming a computer company – in contrast to Remington-Rand. IBM focused on fully understanding the technology and helping customers gain the benefits that computers could provide. They didn't just sell computers. They came to be known as the company that solved customers' information processing problems.

This commitment helped IBM to deal with very substantial challenges. Watson Jr. reflects on these challenges noting that, by 1956, RCA and GE were entering the computer business. RCA was 50% bigger than IBM, and GE was 500% bigger. However, despite this size – or perhaps because of it – these industrial giants did not, or could not, make the type of commitment made by IBM.

This is an excellent example of the organic nature of enterprises. RCA and GE, as well as Remington-Rand, could not remake themselves in the ways necessary. These diverse businesses had too many stakeholders, with a wide variety of interests, to be able to focus in the way possible for IBM. In contrast, IBM had little choice since information processing was its business and computer-based information processing was moving quickly. IBM had to move quickly also, as evidenced, for example, by abandoning vacuum tubes and committing themselves to transistors in the mid-1950s.

Transistors were invented by John Bardeen, Walter Brattain, and William Shockley at Bell Labs in 1947. Bell Labs played a major role in computing and communications research (Gertner, 2012). John Pierce at Bell Labs invented the communications satellite, Telstar, in 1962. The lab was also involved in the computer networking community, which culminated in the ARPANET in 1969, funded by the Advanced Research Projects Agency. I revisit these technologies in Chapter 5.

Watson chronicles the development of the IBM System/360. This was the first computer that I used. It was the fall of 1966 and I was enrolled in a sophomore Fortran programming course. Punch cards were the media. In contrast, at the moment, I am using a MacBook Air laptop with enough memory and disk storage to keep me quite content. Clearly, much has happened in the computer industry in recent decades, not the least of which is that my laptop, as well as my previous laptops, were not produced by IBM.

The System/360 development was driven by a need to replace eight computers in IBM's catalog with an integrated solution. IBM also needed a bold move to bolster growth, as well as compete with Burroughs, GE, Honeywell, and RCA whose current machines were all superior to the existing IBM product lines.

IBM planned to announce the System/360 in April 1964. They met this deadline. However, it required that some of the equipment in the showroom be mockups rather than actual equipment. They started shipping the System/360 in 1965. Soon the backlog of orders became staggering and delays mounted. By the end of 1966, however, production and delivery were going smoothly.

Fisher and colleagues assert that IBM's commitment of substantial corporate resources to uncertain, risky investments such as the 360 illustrates a primary reason for IBM's continual success. The results of this commitment were substantial. Just prior to the System/360 rollout in 1965, IBM had 11,000 computer systems installed. By the time the 370 – the 360's replacement – was announced in 1970, the number had tripled to 35,000. IBM's multi-billion dollar investment had yielded fantastic rewards. Fisher reports that several commentators characterized the 360 investment decision as perhaps the biggest ever in terms of its impact on an American company, bigger than Boeing's decision to go into jets or Ford's decision to proceed with the Mustang.

The other players in the computer industry had a variety of reactions to the System/360. Burroughs responded with a new product line. CDC reduced prices. GE focused on price reductions rather than performance superiority, while also investing in developing time sharing. Honeywell focused on creating a family of systems. RCA reduced prices and announced a competitive system. SDS emphasized the product family approach. Sperry Rand focused on leapfrogging the 360 in terms of performance. By the mid to late 1970s, GE, RCA, and SDS were gone from the market for the reasons elaborated on earlier.

There were, however, new entries in the computer market with a totally new type of offering – minicomputers. The first minicomputer company was Digital Equipment Corporation (DEC) in 1957, the history of which I discuss in the next section. Wang entered the market in 1964. Interdata was founded in 1966 and acquired by Perkin-Elmer in 1974. Hewlett-Packard entered the market in 1967, Data General in 1968, Datapoint in 1969, Prime Computer in 1971, Harris Corporation in 1971, and Tandem in 1974.

A whole new segment of the computer market emerged. IBM dismissed and then ignored this segment. They apparently could not imagine that customers would want to do their own computing rather than have IBM support and possibly staff a centralized computing function. Later IBM tried to catch up but did so poorly.

IBM also had to play catch up in personal computing, which I discuss later in the context of Apple Computer. As with minicomputers, they could not imagine much of a market for microcomputers. They eventually responded with a competitive offering. However, success was short-lived as computer hardware, particularly microprocessors, became commodity items cloned and produced all over the world – a commodity trap situation. Price became the dominant issue.

As the profit margins for computer hardware plummeted, IBM found itself in trouble and lost a lot of money. There were (and are) still profits to be made in software, but IBM's infrastructure is that of a hardware company in general, and a direct sales and customer support company in particular. They have been caught in a paradigm shift from large mainframe, centralized computing to small desktop, distributed computing. Many other companies have also been caught in this shift – for example, vendors of mainframe software systems for accounting, inventory control, and so on.

The result has been substantial downsizing for IBM, as well as the remaining players in the traditional computer industry. Symbolic of this change is the end of the Watson line of leadership at IBM whereby internal candidates were selected and groomed to lead the company. Under Louis V. Gerstner, CEO from 1993 to 2002, IBM came to recognize the commodity nature and price sensitivity of its markets.

Gerstner's strategy was to use processes and culture to regain an advantage. Moving from proprietary standards to open standards was important to his strategy, and the ramifications for processes and culture were enormous. He realized that customers wanted solutions, and did not need to know what equipment their solution ran on. His transformation journey is chronicled in his book *Who Says Elephants Can't Dance?* (Gerstner, 2009).

Interactive Computing – DEC

The seeds of this change were sown over several decades ago. Ken Olsen, working initially with Jay Forrester at MIT, and eventually with IBM, on the SAGE project, envisioned people being in control of their own computing. They would not have to wait for the EDP (electronic data processing) function to process their requests and give them their results. They would see processing and results as they happened. Olsen's vision was heresy in the world of large mainframe computers produced by IBM, UNIVAC, and Burroughs. Hence, these players dismissed his ideas.

The result of Olsen's vision was the formation of Digital Equipment Corporation (DEC) in 1957 with Harlan Anderson. The formation and evolution of DEC are chronicled by Glenn Rifkin and George Harrar in *The Ultimate Entrepreneur* (1988), as well as Jamie Parker Pearson in *Digital at Work* (1992). These chronicles begin with Olsen and Anderson giving up 70% of the equity in their company in order to get $70,000 in venture capital from American Research and Development (ARD).

ARD offered three pieces of advice. First, they cautioned them not to say that they wanted to build computers because – as noted earlier – RCA and GE were both losing money on computers at the time. They suggested that Olsen and Anderson say that they wanted to build printed circuit modules. While Olsen and Anderson wanted to call the company Digital Computer Corporation, this advice led to them naming it Digital Equipment Corporation.

Second, ARD encouraged them to promise more profit than available via investing in the big players. They promised 10%. Finally, they urged them to promise a quick profit. They promised profit in the first year.

In late 1962, DEC won a breakthrough order for 15 PDP-1s from ITT. With the introduction of the PDP-8 in 1965, DEC had defined an industry and grew between 25% and 40% per year in revenues as well as profits for the next 17 years. More than 50,000 PDP-8s were sold in its 15-year lifespan.

I have a special place in my heart for the PDP-8. I did my Ph.D. dissertation using a PDP-8 – serial no. 50 – at MIT. We had tape drive no. 4. With 4,096 words of memory and 12-bit words, assembly language was the only realistic choice for my study of air traffic controllers' abilities to predict aircraft trajectories. Several years ago, my daughter saw a PDP-8 in the Smithsonian and found it quite amusing that I had once worked on a computer that is now in a museum.

Rifkin and Harrar discuss the origin of the word "minicomputer." John Leng, reporting on sales in the UK in 1964, commented, "Here is the latest minicomputer activity in the land of miniskirts as I drive around in my Mini Minor." The age of the minicomputer was born. There were about 70 companies manufacturing minicomputers by 1970.

Not all of DEC's progress was as smooth as with the PDP-8. In 1966, DEC engineers revived the defunct PDP-6 to create the DECsystem10, without Olsen realizing that he had approved this revival. By the early 1970s, the DECsystem10 was a substantial success, ushering many people like myself into time-shared computing. Olsen apparently had a difficult time accepting this new computing paradigm. Nevertheless, the DECsystem10 helped DEC to prosper.

In 1967, Edison de Castro proposed a 16-bit machine that was shot down by Olsen as too advanced. In the spring of 1968, de Castro left with Henry Burkhardt and Dick Sogge to form Data General which introduced a 16-bit computer long before DEC. As a result, DEC's revenues tapered off in 1970 and 1971. While analysts blamed the weaknesses on the recession, DEC knew that their lateness in getting into the 16-bit market had resulted in customers going with Data General and other minicomputer manufacturers. The PDP-11, DEC's 16-bit entry, was two years late but came to stand atop the minicomputer market and eventually sold 250,000 units.

However, by 1975, DEC's product lines of 8s, 10s, and 11s were getting very old – only the PDP-11 was less than five years old. DEC's Gordon Bell was pushing the VAX line. Networking, via DECnet and later Ethernet, was the key to success for the VAX. With the 32-bit VAX, DEC leapfrogged the competition.

DEC outflanked IBM by building small computers. Everyone else – Burroughs, Control Data, Honeywell, NCR, and UNIVAC – tried to grab portions of IBM's own territory in mainframe computers. In 1976, IBM finally introduced a minicomputer.

On the other hand, DEC branched slowly into commercial markets. They found that customer expectations had already been set by IBM and others who provided 100% hand-holding to their customers. DEC was not prepared to provide this level of support. By the late 1970s, DECmate was failing and Wang was walking away with the word processing market.

Also by the late 1970s, Apple was putting the finishing touches on the first personal computer which would spark a new industry. Rifkin and Harrar note that Apple's "opportunity was vast in part because DEC and Olsen, in a classic business oversight, failed to take interactive computing to its next logical step – personal computing – and thus left the field open to (Apple)."

Olsen stubbornly claimed that personal computers would never succeed. However, Dan Bricklin created Visicalc for the Apple II, and sales of the Apple II took off. In August 1981, IBM introduced the IBM PC. This announcement rocked DEC, in part because IBM outsourced about 80% of the machine and, therefore, was able to enter the market very quickly.

The fatal error for DEC was allowing IBM to preempt the marketplace uncontested for a full year. This disadvantage was furthered by the introduction of Lotus 1-2-3 for the PC. DEC lost about $1B trying to get into the personal computer market. Soon, all non-IBM clones, except for Apple, fell by the wayside. By 1984, DEC was out of the personal computer business and remained out for almost ten years.

In 1984, AT&T tried to acquire or merge with DEC. Olsen finally backed out. The introduction of the VAX8600 put DEC ahead again. By 1985, networking had put DEC back on top and AT&T came courting again. DEC was estimated as having taken $2B in sales away from IBM in 1986. However, by 1988 DEC was fighting SUN and Unix in the workstation market.

By the early 1990s, AT&T had acquired NCR. DEC was again in trouble. Distributed computing, based on low-cost, desktop personal computers, made DEC an expensive solution. Severe cost-cutting and layoffs did not stem the losses and Olsen was replaced by Robert B. Palmer. DEC slipped from number two, behind IBM, to number three behind Hewlett-Packard. DEC went through substantial organizational changes in an attempt to redefine itself.

Intel acquired Digital Semiconductor in 1997, the division of DEC that I worked with closely for many years, planning Alpha chips. DEC as a whole was acquired by Compaq Computer in 1998, which was acquired by Hewlett-Packard in 2002. It felt like the end of an era.

What happened to Ken Olsen and DEC? It strikes me that Ken Olsen's vision quest eventually became a paradigm lost situation. There was substantial warning. Olsen's initial reluctance to pursue the DECsystem10 and the 16-bit PDP-11 are examples. His dismissal of the potential of personal computing is perhaps the most telling.

Thus, we see that there were early warning signals for both IBM and DEC. However, we see these with 100% hindsight. How could we know in advance? At the very least, how could we know as soon as such patterns have emerged? What should we look for? What are the key indicators of current situations, and what are the leading indicators of emergent situations?

Personal Computing – Apple

In discussing interactive computing, I noted that Ken Olsen and DEC dismissed and therefore missed personal computing. Instead of DEC, Apple Computer became synonymous with personal computing. The story of Apple is told by Steven Levy in his book *Insanely Great* (1994). This title reflects the ubiquitous use of hyperbole that characterized Steve Jobs, half of the team of Jobs and Wozniak that founded Apple.

Levy chronicles the emergence and evolution of Apple's Macintosh, including the adoption of its features and benefits throughout the personal computer industry. This chronicle begins with Vannevar Bush's 1945 *Atlantic* article "As We May Think." Levy argues that this article sparked the chain reaction that led to the Macintosh almost 40 years later.

This chain of events began when Douglas C. Engelbart read Bush's article while stationed with the Navy in the Philippines. This event, Levy reports, planted the seed for the Macintosh. I can imagine that Ken Olsen, and surely many others, were very much aware of Bush's article. However, Engelbart found the vision offered by Bush to be particularly compelling. I return to Bush's vision in the next chapter.

Was this the point at which the emergence of a silent war situation, and eventually a paradigm-loss situation, was inevitable? The case for this conclusion is very difficult to make because there were a plethora of comparable visions articulated in the years following Bush's article. Thus, it is impossible to argue that this signal event in 1945 is the key to later problems for IBM and DEC. These companies actually missed many signals over very many years.

Nevertheless, Engelbart was motivated. In 1963, now working at SRI (Stanford Research Institute), he published a paper titled "A Conceptual Framework for Augmentation of Man's Intellect." This paper outlines his vision for personal computing. Within this framework, Engelbart invented windows and the mouse. He unveiled his entire system at the Joint Computer Conference in 1968.

Engelbart's major patron for this work was ARPA (Advanced Research Projects Agency) within the Department of Defense. In particular, the Information Processing Techniques Office (IPTO) within ARPA, which was then headed by J.C.R. Licklider, who plays a role in the next chapter as well. Licklider supported a wide range of software-related exploratory and advanced R&D. The seed monies provided by ARPA/IPTO contributed significantly to the successful commercialization of word processing, personal computing, desktop publishing, and spreadsheets.

Levy contrasts the commercial impact of ARPA with that of NASA. He notes that ARPA's *millions* led to software products such as just described. In contrast, NASA's *billions* led to Tang and Teflon. Thus, the government's role and success in contributing to commercial products is mixed.

I have worked with these two agencies for many years, most recently in advisory capacities and, in the past, as an R&D contractor. ARPA is able to get "more bangs for the buck" because they focus on seeding technological innovation. The agency is quite small – in terms of personnel, not budget – and very lean, certainly by government standards and perhaps by commercial standards.

NASA, in contrast, views commercial technological innovation as a by-product. They invest most of their budget in building and operating space shuttles and a space station. With the exception of the much smaller aeronautics side of NASA, this agency's mission is to explore space, not to seed the commercial industry. The somewhat confusing role of the government in technological innovation is further discussed in several chapters.

ARPA's funding of SRI and Engelbart ended in 1975. As often happens when government funding disappears, the SRI team folded. Most of the team went to Xerox's fledging Palo Alto Research Center (PARC). Engelbart went to Tymshare who had bought his augmentation system. Engelbart's vision quest had clearly transitioned to an evolutionary situation.

The next episode on the path toward personal computing happened at Xerox PARC. The Center was established in 1970 to help Xerox gain an advantage in the computer business after, as noted earlier, buying Scientific Data Systems. In the early 1970s, the Alto computer emerged at PARC. Alto features included WYSIWYG (What You See Is What You Get) display presentations that greatly facilitate document preparation and management. The Alto also had a bit-mapped display that enabled its graphical user interface.

The Alto led to the Xerox Star, which emerged as the embodiment of the desktop metaphor. This metaphor would eventually come to dominate the personal computer market. However, Xerox would not be the beneficiary of this success. Douglas K. Smith and Robert C. Alexander in *Fumbling the Future* (1988) argue that Xerox blew a tremendous opportunity, in part due to politics and timidity. Another major factor was the Star's substantial price tag – $18,000 for a basic model. Levy suggests that the lack of cost consciousness was affected by the scientists at Xerox PARC proceeding as if they were working with ARPA grants, not corporate funds.

The culture at Apple was quite different. The ethic was: "If it didn't hit the streets, it wasn't worth doing." The Apple II was introduced in 1977. It soon became a hit, in terms of price, portability, and ease of use.

We bought our first Apple II computers in 1980 in conjunction with a project to build desktop training simulators. I can easily recall my first efforts with the Apple II. I had developed and evaluated a computer-based training concept using a DECsystem 10 as the computer platform. I read the Apple II manual and converted the simulation software to run on the Apple II in one day – that's ease of use!

Apple tried to follow the Apple II with the Lisa which was introduced in 1983. Lisa was created by engineers and managers lured away from Hewlett-Packard. Lisa enabled direct manipulation, had pull-down menus, and employed icons on a desktop manager. If Lisa had cost half as much and been several times as fast, it might have succeeded in the market. While we were committed users of Apple IIs, we never considered or even looked at the Lisa.

In December 1979, Steve Jobs and his Apple colleagues visited Xerox PARC. Levy concludes that they left with the paradigm that was to become the Macintosh. The Macintosh project was formalized in 1982 and became Steve Jobs' pet project. On January 22, 1984, Apple's infamous Superbowl ad launched the Mac.

The Mac with 128K words of memory was far ahead of its predecessors but was nevertheless deficient. Its bit-mapped display needed more memory than envisioned. Fortunately, memory was increasingly cheap. However, these two considerations were overlooked. Further, producing software for the Mac was several orders of magnitude more difficult than for less sophisticated systems. Easy to use, hard to program was the general conclusion, as well as the feelings of my company's software staff.

The 1984 sales did not live up to projections. The shortfall in sales resulted in a power struggle between Steve Jobs and John Sculley. Sculley had been hired from Pepsi to serve as President, the idea being that greater consumer orientation was needed at Apple. The power struggle resulted in Jobs being fired by the Board of Directors in May of 1985.

The memory limitations of the Mac were easy to remedy. More importantly, in retrospect, Apple decided that its printers would produce documents using PostScript from Adobe. When Aldus' desktop publishing software PageMaker became available for the Mac in July 1985, Apple had an application for which it was worth buying a computer. The Mac became increasingly successful.

Another Mac application that became quite popular was HyperCard, and later SuperCard. The card paradigm and the ability to define links among cards to create what is called hypertext was pioneered by Ted Nelson. Interestingly, Nelson was another enthusiast of Vannevar Bush's ideas. Thus, the Mac's success was based on several innovative applications.

However, despite a late start, IBM was still the leader. IBM passed up the chance to buy the fledgling company that later became Xerox. IBM also failed to recognize the markets for minicomputers and microcomputers. However, IBM's PCs (personal computers) finally provided an excuse for corporate data processing executives to begin purchasing desktop computers. While Apple had the technology and ease of use on its side, IBM had the installed base of customers and relationships in the business world.

IBM selected Bill Gates and Microsoft to create the software operating system for its PC. The result was DOS (disk operating system). With IBM's huge market presence, DOS became the de facto standard despite its inferiority to the Mac's easy-to-use interface. At the same time, a commodity trap situation was emerging for personal computer hardware.

To compete with DOS's seemingly insurmountable lead, Sculley at Apple had to either license the Mac operating system to others or sharply lower the Mac's price. He hesitated on the price cut until 1990. It was too late to stem the PC tide. Levy concludes that this delay may have ultimately cost Sculley his job.

While the Mac faltered, the PowerBook – a laptop – was introduced in 1991. Apple sold a billion dollars' worth of PowerBooks in the first year. The concept of the PowerBook can be traced to Alan Kay who was influenced by Dave Evans and Ivan Sutherland at the University of Utah and Seymour Papert at MIT. Based on Papert's computer language LOGO, Kay and his colleagues at PARC in the 1970s developed the language Smalltalk, as well as the concept of overlapping windows. Their vision of the ultimate laptop was called the Dynabook. Almost 20 years later, the PowerBook emerged, providing yet another example of a vision quest becoming an evolution situation.

At about the same time that Mac was stumbling and the PowerBooks were booming, Sculley introduced the Knowledge Navigator. Levy characterizes this concept as Sculley's personal mixture of everybody else's visions. In a brief, but very compelling video, Apple painted the picture beyond laptops. At center stage in this picture was the Knowledge Navigator, an example of a Personal Digital Assistant (PDA).

To focus on PDAs, Apple participated in the formation of General Magic, a venture with AT&T, Matsushita, Motorola, Philips, and Sony. On its own, Apple focused on the Apple Newton and related PDAs. The evolution of the Newton is reported by John Markoff in his article "Marketer's Dream, Engineer's Nightmare" in the *New York Times* (1993).

Markoff begins by recounting Sculley's sweeping claims about the functionality of the Newton and its likely impact on the marketplace. He argues that Sculley – Apple's self-proclaimed technologist – promised the market too much too fast. His eager boosterism also encouraged other companies to pursue competitive products much sooner than they might have, providing Apple with more competition faster.

The Newton started in 1987 with an individual engineer's vision of a PDA. A team was soon formed to create the Newton. Markoff argues that Sculley was never able to form a relationship with this team. In fact, via his commitment to General Magic, Sculley encouraged development of a competing product.

As indicated earlier, Sculley was at this time involved in fierce price wars. Needing a new product success and needing it soon, he supported the Newton team in exchange for a promise to have the product in the market by April, 1992. With only a two-year time budget, the team scaled back its vision. The original $8,000 machine was scaled back initially to $4,000 and eventually to less than $1,000. This scaling back required the elimination of wireless communication as well as knowledge-based decision support. Only handwriting recognition remained of the original leading-edge functionality.

A demo of a prototype Newton was shown at an electronics trade show in May 1992. It was discovered, however, that the language upon which the Newton's software was to be based had to be scrapped. This led to slipping the release of the Newton until the summer of 1993. In the process, many additional features were dropped. When the Newton finally appeared, even its premier feature – language recognition – worked poorly. The Newton soon became grist for cartoonists and comedians.

Initial sales of the Newton were very disappointing. This disappointment, in combination with the aforementioned hesitancy to cut Mac prices to maintain market share, resulted in Sculley's stock plummeting. He was forced out in 1993 and replaced by Michael Spindler whose forte was operations rather than marketing.

This case study of Apple provides insights into vision quest situations and how they can go awry. The Apple II and the Mac provide examples of visions realized. The Apple II was an unqualified market success, while the success of the Mac did not meet expectations. Nevertheless, both products were thought of very highly.

The failure of the Mac to sell in the volumes sought resulted in Apple having to scramble. Sculley's vision was very appealing. When I first saw the Knowledge Navigator video, I was intrigued. My colleagues and I watched it again and again. As developers of computer-based decision support systems, we debated which elements of the Knowledge Navigator were just around the corner and which were more speculative.

For us, this video provided a signpost in the evolution situation which we were experiencing. In contrast, Sculley it appears, as well as others at Apple, believed they could create a slimmed-down version of the Knowledge Navigator now. The Newton and other PDA efforts resulted. The problem, however, is that Apple's technology and engineering skills were not up to realizing marketing's visions.

Levy concludes by noting that the lessons learned in the creation of the Mac have affected the entire computer community. Apple was, at the time, no longer doing the teaching. Further, the opportunity to capitalize on the Mac's superiority was lost. However, windows, pull-down menus, the mouse, and so on are now elements of virtually every computing system.

Microsoft Interlude

Levy briefly mentions one very substantial beneficiary of the Mac's contributions – Bill Gates and Microsoft. As noted earlier, Microsoft prospered when IBM chose them to create the operating system software – DOS – for IBM's PC. DOS soon became the industry standard, except for Apple enthusiasts.

Microsoft Windows replaced DOS as the standard, although DOS was still there running underneath Windows until Windows 95 was released. Levy argues that Bill Gates wanted to replace DOS with Windows for two reasons. One reason was a genuine belief that a graphical user interface is better. Apple, with their Mac, had clearly demonstrated that this is what the market wanted.

If the Mac had been less expensive, and perhaps much easier to program, Apple might have had Microsoft's market position. Actually, the same could be said about Xerox. However, Microsoft became the leader, not because they had the best product technically, but because they had a broad market presence – due to the IBM link – and they priced their products more reasonably.

Microsoft wanted to compete in the software applications markets. With the introduction of Windows, Gates reset the clock in the applications competition. Everyone had to create new software packages, even the market leaders in word processing, spreadsheets, databases, and so on. The result was that several Microsoft applications gained significant market share, often bundled together as Microsoft Office.

Most of the computer hardware manufacturers were caught in commodity trap situations. Software offers much better profit potential. I have worked with several computer companies as they have attempted to chart their futures. They all realize that they need to place much greater emphasis on their software offerings, and much less emphasis on their hardware revenues.

They all say this. Yet when you reflect on many of their "gut" decisions, all you can see is hardware. They want to bend metal, not push bits. In part, this is due to a desire to productively employ their investments in manufacturing facilities. However, more important, from my perspective, is their lack of understanding of the situations that they are in and likely future situations.

Digital Devices – Apple Again

In 1997, Steve Jobs returned to Apple as CEO after the company's acquisition of NeXT. He was largely responsible for reviving Apple, which was on the verge of bankruptcy. A steady stream of innovations began with the iPod. The first version was released on October 23, 2001, about eight-and-a-half months after the Macintosh version of iTunes was released. Apple sold an estimated 450 million iPod products as of 2022.

Apple's next innovation transformed the marketplace. The first-generation iPhone was announced by Jobs on January 9, 2007. Over 2.24 billion iPhone units have been sold to date. Apple TV was also launched in 2007. Speaking at Macworld Expo that year, Jobs announced that Apple was dropping the word "Computer" from its name to become "Apple Inc.".

The iPad device was announced and unveiled on January 27, 2010, by Jobs at an Apple press event; 678 million units have been sold. The Apple Watch was released in April 2015 and quickly became the best-selling wearable device: More than 101 million people were estimated to use an Apple Watch as of December 2020. Apple Watch accounted for 34.1% of all smartwatch shipments in 2022, and 60% of the revenue for the entire market, globally.

Isaacson's in-depth biography *Steve Jobs* (2011) provides many insights into these developments. The broad availability of affordable digital devices set the stage for the revolution of the Internet and social media which I address in Chapter 5. First, however, we need to consider the financial, physical, and psychological exploitation enabled by the enormous success of innovations in computing and communications.

EXPLOITATION BY COMPUTING AND COMMUNICATIONS

The enormous growth in this industry has resulted in a range of exploitation, summarized in Table 4.1. Exploitation via "externalities"

TABLE 4.1

Innovation and Exploitation in Computing and Communications

Innovations	Mainframes, minicomputers, microcomputers, and digital devices.
Financial exploitation	Vendor lock-in, high frequency trading, and cryptocurrency.
Physical exploitation	Server emissions, toxic waste, and electronics trash.
Psychological exploitation	Learning curves, failed connections, and inactive lifestyles.
Mitigating exploitation	Regulations, anti-trust laws, and externality taxes.

concerns societal impacts for which manufacturers and service providers are not accountable: Exploiters focus on maximizing efficiency and profits at the expense of the environment, health, and safety. A human-centered society creates mechanisms to counter these tendencies.

Financial Exploitation

There are three types of financial exploitation of interest: vendor lock-in, high frequency trading, and cryptocurrencies. These represent three primary ways to exploit consumers and investors. Inordinate profit is the overarching goal.

Vendor Lock-In. This is a technique used by some technology vendors to make their customers dependent on them for products and services, making it hard to switch to a competitor without substantial costs or difficulty.

Many people have experienced this with regard to Microsoft Windows and Apple's Mac OS. Once you have some level of skill with one of these, and have developed applications on that platform, the cost of switching platforms can be prohibitive.

On a corporate scale, switching costs can be enormous as illustrated in Table 4.2. I have talked to many executives who feel "stuck" with a legacy ERP, CRM, or EHR application and cannot afford the costs of a transition. A common motivation for transitions is acquisition or merger with another firm that uses the other platform.

High Frequency Trading. Advanced computer and communications technologies have enabled exploitation via high frequency trading.

TABLE 4.2

Costs of Major Software Transitions

Application	Vendor Transition	Costs of Transition	Source
ERP (Enterprise Resource Planning)	SAP → Oracle	$50,000–100,000 plus $130–200 per user per month; possibly millions	Crail (2023)
CRM (Customer Relationship Management)	Salesforce → Monday	$25–300 per user per month for Salesforce; $8–16 for Monday	Hughes (2022)
EHR (Electronic Health Records)	Cerner → Epic	$1.5 billion for Mayo Clinic	Kuhrt (2017)

Michael Lewis' *Flash Boys* (2014) explores the scheme whereby traders use ultra-fast network connections to "front run" other, slower traders, thereby acting before others can respond. He argues that high frequency trading creates something akin to predatory insider trading.

Lewis chronicles the endeavors of a small group of Wall Street veterans who realize that the US stock market has been rigged for the benefit of insiders. They band together to investigate, expose, and reform the insidious new ways that Wall Street generates profits. He concludes that broad technological changes and unethical trading practices have transformed the US stock market from "the world's most public, most democratic, financial market" into a "rigged" market.

I encountered this world when I was a faculty member at Stevens Institute of Technology in Hoboken, New Jersey, where more than 30% of its graduates went to work on Wall Street. The CEO of one of these training companies explained the statistical models that enabled their high frequency trading. I asked him how these models included the market position of companies. He responded, "We don't. We are only going to own the stock for a few seconds."

Cryptocurrencies

Advanced computer and communications technologies have also enabled cryptocurrencies – digital money. It does not require a bank or financial institution to verify transactions. It can be used for purchases or as an investment. Transactions are verified and recorded on a blockchain, an unchangeable ledger that tracks and records assets and trades.

Paul Krugman, a well-informed skeptic of the whole concept, concludes that "Cryptocurrencies have made almost no inroads into the traditional role of money. They're too awkward to use for ordinary transactions. Their values are too unstable." (Krugman, 2002). Public trust in crypto has hit rock bottom after a string of high-profile swindles and crashes, notably the downfall of FTX, a popular cryptocurrency exchange (Economist, 2023).

It seems to me that the whole scheme is just another way for technology aficionados to make money. They seek to monetize advanced technologies but avoid the externalities of bitcoin farming.

PHYSICAL EXPLOITATION

Toxic By-Products

Semiconductor manufacturing, so central to computing and communications, creates toxic by-products.

> Health-related lawsuits are bringing high-profile attention to the environmental and occupational effects of what is now the world's largest and fastest growing manufacturing sector. This prodigious economic growth comes with a hefty environmental price tag, however. The semiconductor industry uses large amounts of toxic chemicals to manufacture the components that make up a computer, including disk drives, circuit boards, video display equipment, and silicon chips themselves, the basic building blocks of computer devices. The toxic materials needed to make the (hundreds of) billions of silicon chips manufactured annually are staggering in amount and include highly corrosive hydrochloric acid; metals such as arsenic, cadmium, and lead; volatile solvents such as methyl chloroform, toluene, benzene, acetone, and trichloroethylene; and toxic gases such as arsine. Many of these chemicals are known or probable human carcinogens.
>
> **(Chepesiuk, 1999)**

Electronics Waste

> It's not just computer chips that present environmentally related health problems. Computers themselves are manufactured with and include a number of hazardous materials. Of major concern are platinum in circuit

boards, copper in transformers, nickel and cobalt in disk drives, barium and cadmium coatings on computer glass, and lead solder on circuit boards and video screens. Obsolete computers also require special and often expensive handling to safely dispose of them.

(Chepesiuk, 1999)

E-waste, electronic waste, e-scrap and end-of-life electronics are terms often used to describe used electronics that are nearing the end of their useful life, and are discarded, donated or given to a recycler. Though "e-waste" is the commonly used term, EPA considers e-waste to be a subset of used electronics and recognizes the inherent value of these materials that can be reused, refurbished or recycled to minimize the actual waste that might end up in a landfill or improperly disposed in an unprotected dump site either in the US or abroad.

(EPA, 2022)

Server Farm Emissions

Bitcoin farming creates a range of by-products as well.

Crypto-assets are digital assets that are implemented using cryptographic techniques. Crypto-assets can require considerable amounts of electricity usage, which can result in greenhouse gas emissions, as well as additional pollution, noise, and other local impacts to communities living near mining facilities.

(OSTP, 2022)

Top-down estimates of the electricity consumption of cryptocurrency mining in the United States imply that the industry was responsible for an excess 27.4 million tons of carbon dioxide (CO_2) between mid-2021 and 2022 — or three times as much as emitted by the largest coal plant in the U.S. in 2021.

(Earth Justice, 2023)

Psychological Exploitation

New capabilities result in extended learning curves for new hardware and software, which requires human investments of time and patience. This includes troubleshooting failed connections. To be fair, however, we endure these types of exploitation because we want the benefits of the technologies.

Inactive lifestyles due to extended screen time pose health risks and undermine important competencies. For example, reading levels in the US are steadily declining, especially for children. Reading competencies are central to achievement in science, technology, engineering, and mathematics, as well as most other endeavors.

The greatest psychological exploitation is the impact of misinformation and disinformation, which are enabled by computer and communications technologies, but energized by the Internet and social media. I explore these phenomena in detail in the next chapter.

RESPONSES TO EXPLOITATION

An integrated response to mitigate exploitation is more likely to be enacted rather than piecemeal pieces of legislation having to overcome separate battles. Hence, I propose the following mitigation agenda.

Mitigation Agenda

Legislation and regulations exist to address financial exploitation. The Department of Justice has demonstrated its ability to respond to market exploitation. A good example is the breakup of AT&T. The breakup of the Bell System was mandated on January 8, 1982, by an agreed consent decree providing that AT&T Corporation would, as had been initially proposed by AT&T, relinquish control of the Bell Operating Companies, which had provided local telephone service in the United States.

Another example is the Microsoft suit. The Department of Justice announced on September 6, 2001, that it was no longer seeking to break up Microsoft and would instead seek a lesser anti-trust penalty. Microsoft decided to draft a settlement proposal allowing PC manufacturers to adopt non-Microsoft software.

Much more recently, concerns about the clout and reach of Google, Facebook, Amazon, and Apple have grown. "Without the discipline of meaningful market-based competition, digital platforms may act in ways that are not responsive to consumer demands," observed the head of the Justice Department's anti-trust division. (Wakabayashi et al., 2019).

Legislation will be needed to address, and provide responses to, physical exploitation. Who is responsible for the consequences of societal exploitation and how do they compensate society? Taxation to address externalities would be warranted. These taxes would be paid upon purchase of computer and communications capabilities and perhaps for the annual use of these capabilities. This legislative effort could be led by the EPA.

Role of Government

The charters of the government agencies involved in the mitigation agenda are summarized in Table 4.3. Business practice issues are addressed by the DOJ, FTC, FCC, and SEC. Environment risks are concerns of the EPA.

TABLE 4.3

Selected US Government Agencies

Agency (Founding)	Agency Charter
DOJ (1870)	The United States Department of Justice, also known as the Justice Department, is a federal executive department of the United States government tasked with the enforcement of federal law and administration of justice in the United States. It is equivalent to the justice or interior ministries of other countries.
EPA (1970)	The Environmental Protection Agency is an independent executive agency of the United States federal government tasked with environmental protection matters.
FCC (1934)	The Federal Communications Commission is an independent agency of the United States federal government that regulates communications by radio, television, wire, satellite, and cable across the United States.
FTC (1914)	The Federal Trade Commission is an independent agency of the United States government whose principal mission is the enforcement of civil antitrust law and the promotion of consumer protection. The FTC shares jurisdiction over federal civil antitrust enforcement with the Department of Justice Antitrust Division.
SEC (1934)	The US Securities and Exchange Commission is an independent agency of the United States federal government, created in the aftermath of the Wall Street Crash of 1929. The primary purpose of the SEC is to enforce the law against market manipulation.

CONCLUSIONS

The creative balancing of business innovation and societal exploitation requires understanding the dynamics of technological innovation and the inevitable exploitation motivated by the pursuit of success. This balance should be thoughtfully monitored and managed. This includes paying careful attention to emerging trends.

The emergence of large language models in artificial intelligence (AI), e.g., ChatGPT, has raised concerns about how this technology might lead to societal exploitation. There have been proposals that we should pursue augmented rather than automated intelligence (Rouse & Spohrer, 2018). There has also been substantial articulation of the notion of human-AI teaming (NAP, 2021). In general, the broad notion of human-centered AI has received considerable attention (Shneiderman, 2022).

This is challenging and risky because the inevitable hype dominates and leads to inflated expectations. Riches are seen as just around the corner. Many innovations then enter a "valley of death" period. Some eventually emerge to provide substantial benefits but also motivate inevitable exploitive tendencies. A human-centered society understands these phenomena and creates mechanisms to manage them.

REFERENCES

Chepesiuk, R. (1999). Where the chips fall. *Environmental Health Perspectives*, 107 (9), 453–457.

Cortada, J.W. (1993). *Before the Computer: IBM, NCR, Burroughs, and Remington Rand and the Industry They Created, 1865–1956*. Princeton, NJ: Princeton University Press.

Crail, C. (2023). SAP vs. Oracle 2023 ERP Comparison. *Forbes*. www.forbes.com. May 12.

Earth Justice. (2023). The environmental impacts of cryptomining. *Earth Justice*. https://earthjustice.org/feature/cryptocurrency-mining-environmental-impacts.

EPA. (2022). *Cleaning Up Electronic Waste (E-Waste)*. https://www.epa.gov/international-cooperation/cleaning-electronic-waste-e-waste.

Fisher, F.M., McKie, J.W., & Mancke, R.B. (1983). *IBM and the U.S. Data Processing Industry: An Economic History*. New York: Praeger.

Gerstner, L.V. (2009). *Who Says Elephants Can't Dance?: Leading a Great Enterprise Through Dramatic Change*. New York: HarperCollins.

Gertner, J. (2012). *The Idea Factory: Bell Labs and the Great Age of American Innovation*. New York: Penguin.

Grosvenor, E.S., & Wesson, M. (2016). *Alexander Graham Bell*. San Francisco, CA: New World City.

Hughes, J. (2022). Monday.com vs Salesforce compared. *The Digital Merchant*, August 11.

Isaacson, W. (2003). *Benjamin Franklin: An American Life*. New York: Simon & Schuster.

Isaacson, W. (2011). *Steve Jobs*. New York: Simon & Schuster.

Isaacson, W. (2014). *The Innovators: How a Group of Hackers, Geniuses, and Geeks Created the Digital Revolution*. New York: Simon & Schuster.

Jonnes, J. (2003). *Empires of Light: Edison, Tesla, Westinghouse and the Race to Electrify the World*. New York: Random House.

Krugman, P. (2022). Is this the end game for crypto? *New York Times*, November 17.

Kuhrt, M. (2017). Mayo clinic health system begins $1.5B EHR rollout, moving from Cerner, GE, to Epic system. *Fierce Healthcare*, July 14.

Levy, S. (1994). *Insanely Great: The Life and Times of Macintosh, the Computer That Changed Everything*. New York: Viking.

Lewis, M. (2014). *Flash Boys: A Wall Street Revolt*. New York: Norton.

Macrae, N. (1992). *John von Neumann: The Scientific Genius Who Pioneered the Modern Computer, Game Theory, Nuclear Deterrence, and Much More*. New York: Pantheon.

Maney, K. (2003). *The Maverick and His Machine: Thomas H. Watson Sr. and the Making of IBM*. New York: Wiley.

Markoff, J. (1993). Marketer's dream, engineer's nightmare. *New York Times*, December 12.

NAP. (2021). *Human-AI Teaming: State of the Art and Research Needs*. Washington, DC: National Academies Press.

OSTP. (2022). *Fact Sheet: Climate and Energy Implications of Crypto-Assets in the United States*. Washington, DC: Office of Science and Technology Policy.

Rifkin, G., & Harrar, G. (1988). *The Ultimate Entrepreneur: The Story of Ken Olsen and Digital Equipment Corporation*. Chicago, IL: Contemporary Books.

Rouse, W.B., & Spohrer, J.C. (2018). Automating versus augmenting intelligence. *Journal of Enterprise Transformation*. https://doi.org/10.1080/19488289.2018.1424059.

Shneiderman, B. (2022). *Human-Centered AI*. Oxford: Oxford University Press.

The Economist. (2023). The promise of crypto has not lived up to its initial excitement. *The Economist*, May 15.

Wakabayashi, D., Benner, K., & Lohr, S. (2019). Justice department opens antitrust review of big tech companies. *New York Times*, July 23.

Watson, T.J. Jr. (1990). *Father, Son & Co.* New York: Bantam.

5

Internet and Social Media

The technological developments chronicled in Chapter 4 provided the foundation for the Internet and subsequently social media. The benefits of these innovations have been enormous, for example for coping with the pandemic. The exploitive consequences of the Internet and social media include those discussed in Chapter 4 plus surveillance capitalism and the infodemic of misinformation and disinformation. These consequences are particularly challenging.

INNOVATION IN INTERNET AND SOCIAL MEDIA

The innovations in computing and communications outlined in Chapter 4 occurred over centuries. In contrast, the innovations in the Internet and social media are much more recent. The beginning, it can be argued, commenced with the end of World War II. Many of the innovations that I discuss in this section are also chronicled by Isaacson (2014).

Thought Leadership

Vannevar Bush set the tone with "As We May Think," published in *The Atlantic* in 1945. Of particular relevance to this chapter is a concept he termed "Memex."

> A memex is a device in which an individual stores all his books, records, and communications, and which is mechanized so that it may be consulted with exceeding speed and flexibility. It is an enlarged intimate supplement

to his memory. The matter of bulk is well taken care of by improved microfilm.

(Bush, 1945)

His thinking was sound even if microfilm would not be the eventual media.

J.C.R. Licklider gained the mantle of thought leadership from Bush, both being MIT faculty members. His classic article "Man-Computer Symbiosis," published in *IEEE Transactions* in 1960 presaged contemporary developments.

Man-computer symbiosis is an expected development in cooperative interaction between men and electronic computers. It will involve very close coupling between the human and the electronic members of the partnership. The main aims are 1) to let computers facilitate formulative thinking as they now facilitate the solution of formulated problems, and 2) to enable men and computers to cooperate in making decisions and controlling complex situations without inflexible dependence on prede-termined programs. In the anticipated symbiotic partnership, men will set the goals, formulate the hypotheses, determine the criteria, and perform the evaluations. Computing machines will do the routinizable work that must be done to prepare the way for insights and decisions in technical and scientific thinking.

(Licklider, 1960)

His thinking came together in *Libraries of the Future* (Licklider, 1965), a study of what libraries might be at the end of the twentieth century. Licklider's book reviewed systems for information storage, organization, and retrieval, the use of computers in libraries, and library question-answering systems. This book appealed to computer scientists and engineers rather than librarians. I read it in 1969, when first at MIT. I bought it at the annual sale of MIT Press and found it compelling.

The state of the art has obviously evolved enormously. I will outline and illustrate the current state later in this chapter, after I relate the technological innovations between the 1960s and recent times, six decades later.

Infrastructure

A few key pieces of the puzzle emerged in the 1960s and 70s. As noted in Chapter 4, the communication satellite, Telstar, was invented at Bell Labs by John Pierce in 1962. The Advanced Research Projects Agency (ARPA) funded the development and deployment of ARPANET during 1969–1971, led by none other than J.C.R. Licklider, as head of the Information Processing Techniques Office (IPTO).

The Global Positioning System (GPS) is a space-based radio-navigation system, owned by the US Government and operated by the United States. Roger Eaton, Ivan Getting, and Brad Parkinson are credited with its development in 1973. GPS was approved for commercial use by President Clinton in 1996.

Transmission Control Protocol/Internet Protocol (TCP/IP) was formulated by Robert Kahn and Vinton Cerf in 1973, and funded by ARPA. It was published in *IEEE Transactions* in 1974. Cerf has worked for Google as a vice president and Chief Internet Evangelist since October 2005.

Cell Phones

Motorola demonstrated the first cell phone in 1973. They had great market success with the Flip phone in 1995 and the Razr phone in 2005. They struggled to compete with Nokia, which had a 39% market share in 2008.

In 2012, Google acquired Motorola Mobility for $12.5 billion to gain Motorola Mobility's patent portfolio and protect other Android vendors from litigation. Google sold Motorola Mobility to Lenovo for $2.91 billion, retaining the patent portfolio.

As I discussed in Chapter 4, Apple brought the iPhone to market in 2007. Despite its $500 price, it was an instant success.

> Beginning in 2007, (traditional mobile phones) are rapidly replaced by the pocket-size smartphone, granting full access to music, media, and the internet. Smartphones further host countless utilities that enhance every-day life, including a camera that shoots high-quality photos and video. Oh, and it also makes phone calls. The smartphone may be the single greatest invention in the history of inventions.
>
> **(Tyson, 2022)**

Internet Services

The internet was transitioned from ARPA to the National Science Foundation in 1980. "The World Wide Web, invented in 1989 by British computer scientist Tim Berners-Lee at the European Organization for

Nuclear Research (CERN) in Switzerland became ubiquitous in the 1990s" (Tyson, 2022).

Dial-up America Online was launched in 1993. Netscape was founded under the name Mosaic Communications Corporation in 1994, the brainchild of Jim Clark who had recruited Marc Andreessen as co-founder. The Netscape browser motivated Microsoft to create Internet Explorer in 1995. By 2010, Microsoft was forced by the European Commission to allow users of its Windows operating system to choose different browsers.

The internet bubble emerged during 1995–2000. During this period, the Nasdaq Composite stock market index rose 800%, only to fall 740% when the bubble burst. I remember this starkly as the order book for the software and services we were selling to top technology companies evaporated overnight. These companies eliminated all discretionary spending. Fortunately, increased government demand for our research services kept us afloat.

Consumer Services

Amazon (1994) was founded by Jeff Bezos as an online bookstore. It now sells and delivers almost everything, often in one day. The big box retailers such as Target and Walmart have created online capabilities in the wake of Amazon's success.

Google (1998) was founded by Sergey Brin and Larry Page, based on their PageRank search engine technology that measures the importance of webpages based on the links pointing to them. Google's revenue is dominated by advertising on the pages resulting from searches.

Myspace (2003) was founded by Tom Anderson and Chris DeWolfe as a social networking service. The site was the first social network to reach a global audience and had a significant influence on technology, pop culture, and music. Failing to innovate, they were eclipsed by Facebook.

Facebook (2004) was founded by Mark Zuckerberg and several partners to enable Harvard students to post photographs of themselves and personal information about their lives. Facebook's revenue is dominated by advertising on the pages resulting from searches. Outrageous posts and "likes" drive hits, which determine advertising rates.

Twitter (also known as X) (2006) was founded by Jack Dorsey and partners as a social network that enables users to post texts, photos, and videos known as "tweets." Twitter's revenue is also dominated by advertising. Rates are increased by retweets. Elon Musk purchased Twitter in 2022. The platform has lately been criticized for an increase in content involving hate speech.

Instagram (2010) was founded by Kevin Systrom as a photo- and video-sharing social media platform. Advertising is its primary source of revenue. Facebook acquired Instagram in 2012. Instagram accounts for roughly half of Facebook's revenue.

TikTok (2016) was launched by Chinese company ByteDance to enable users to create and share short videos, with functionality that makes the platform more participatory and fun. TikTok generates revenue when brands buy ads to reach their worldwide audiences.

With the exception of Amazon, the revenue of all of these consumer services companies is dominated by advertising. Spending by advertisers on social media is projected to reach almost $300 billion in 2023. That amounts to roughly $60 for each of the five billion users of social media.

Curis Meditor

David Seuss, CEO of Northern Light, and I created a contemporary vision of the capabilities heralded by Bush and Licklider. We named it *Curis Meditor* (www.CurisMeditor.com), which is Latin for "health best practices." It is hosted on Northern Light's SinglePoint platform.

Capabilities

Our intent is to provide knowledge to enhance the health of people, processes, organizations, and society. There is a series of tailored dashboards, each developed for sponsors of a current or former research project.

- Innovation landscape
- Healthcare industry
- Public health policy
- Cancer control
- Opioid epidemic
- Assistive technology
- Healthcare data sets

- Computational models
- Systems research

Systems Research includes four more dashboards

- Systems science
- Systems engineering
- Software engineering
- Operations research

Each dashboard provides access to daily content on contemporary developments, as well as a variety of expert searches formulated by subject matter experts.

The searches provide access to curated content; for *Curis Meditor*, ten million published articles in four corpora: News, Scientific Research, Conference Abstracts, and Thought Leaders. News includes access to 50,000 English-language articles published globally each day.

It is interesting to contrast *Curis Meditor* with *Google*. A search on *Curis Meditor* will typically result in 500–1,000 curated publications. *Google* will usually yield 100–500 million hits. *Curis Meditor* is only searching curated content. *Google* searches the whole Internet for anything at all related to the search query.

Research Process

The research process supported by *Curis Meditor* is summarized in Figure 5.1. The queries vary, of course, but the searches and analyses employ similar methods. The process is applied to the aforementioned corpus of ten million documents – 8.2 million research articles, 1.4 million news articles, and 13,000 thought leader publications.

The queries of these highly curated corpora result in the identification of hundreds of highly rated documents. The Northern Light machine learning function *Insights* "reads" these documents and provides summaries in the context of the stated query. *Insights* that are particularly promising can be further pursued with the *More Like This* function. One can quite quickly digest an enormous corpus of research findings.

Quite recently, Northern Light has added access to Chap GPT. SinglePoint poses the search query as a question to Chat GPT. It responds with prose

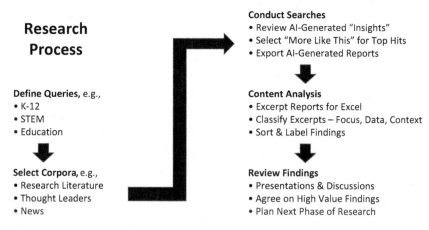

FIGURE 5.1.
Overall research process

answers, that seem pretty reasonable to me. To test its credibility, I posed questions quite far afield. It responded, "I don't know enough to answer your question." I found it comforting that it did not just wing it.

Case Studies

Two recent case studies illustrate the power of *Curis Meditor*. The first involved formulating a dynamic state-based model of substance abuse to incorporate in a large agent-based model of Washington, DC, for the purpose of exploring the impacts of alternative social interventions on addiction, overdosing, and death.

Curis Meditor was employed to review 250 medical research articles on the dynamics of addiction. Phenomena central to addiction were identified, e.g., overdoses lead to cardio and pulmonary comorbidities. Factors that affect transition probabilities were identified. Interventions that are particularly successful, e.g., peer recovery coaches, were explored. Social determinants that affect addiction and recovery were summarized.

The result was an evidence-based model of the dynamics of addiction with transition probabilities among states defined and ranges determined. Archetypical agents were defined. All of this analysis required just eight hours of work, due to the capabilities of *Curis Meditor*. The overall model and results are reported in Tolk et al. (2023).

More recently, we have explored interventions to enhance K-12 outcomes (Rouse, Lombardi & Gargano, 2023). We employed *Curis Meditor* to access evidence for interventions that have been proven to enhance student outcomes. We found that computer-based games, often embedded in summer camps for K-12 students, were usually effective. This led to a proposal for a specific game to enhance STEM readiness and engagement.

Due to the capabilities of *Curis Meditor*, these analyses involved weeks of effort, not months or longer. The future that Bush and Licklider projected has arrived. It involves capabilities that they might not have envisioned, but I expect they would enthusiastically embrace.

Summary

The last five decades or so have provided a rich harvest of innovations, starting with the infrastructure for the Internet and ending with the onslaught of social media, for better or worse. We are now all connected 24/7, able to access enormous amounts of information and connect to work via Zoom, Teams, Webex, or other capabilities. The pandemic accelerated this transition.

Yet all is not well. There is a dark side to social media, leading to phenomena that we are not fully prepared to address. The innovations have created many billionaires, but there are also huge numbers of disaffected people. We need to understand such phenomena and explore how a human-centered society can best address them.

EXPLOITATIONS BY THE INTERNET AND SOCIAL MEDIA

The Internet and social media rely on the computing and communications technologies discussed in Chapter 4. Thus, the Internet and social media contribute to the exploitations discussed in that chapter. However, I need not repeat the discussion of these relationships, which all come together in Chapter 8.

The enormous growth in this industry has resulted in a range of exploitations, summarized in Table 5.1. Exploitation via "externalities"

TABLE 5.1

Innovation and Exploitation in Internet and Social Media

Innovations	ARPANET, TCP/IP, world wide web, and browsers.
Financial Exploitation	Monopoly pricing and vendor lock-in.
Physical Exploitation	Server emissions, outcomes of bad info and advice, and outrage injuries.
Psychological Exploitation	Misinformation, disinformation, anger, fear, and depression.
Mitigating Exploitation	Regulations, anti-trust laws, media laws, and externality taxes.

concerns societal impacts for which manufacturers and service providers are not accountable: Exploiters focus on maximizing efficiency and profits at the expense of the environment, health, and safety. A human-centered society creates mechanisms to counter these tendencies.

Exploitation of Consumers

The overarching goals of Amazon, Google, Facebook, etc. are to maximize profits and, hence, share prices. Social media companies typically earn most of their revenue from advertising, which typically is calculated from page views by users. Their overarching goal, therefore, is to keep people connected. Outrageous content does this better than mundane postings.

In the process, they capture staggering amounts of data from consumers and members. The result is what Zuboff (2019) terms "surveillance capitalism." This is "a concept in political economics which denotes the widespread collection and commodification of personal data by corporations. This phenomenon is distinct from government surveillance, though the two can reinforce each other" (Zuboff, 2019).

Of course, they use this data to target ads and provide links to content they expect particular users will highly value. How does organic search compare to online ads? "The search condition is associated with slightly higher (consumer) surplus relative to the ad condition." Consumer surplus equals the amount a customer was willing to pay minus the amount the customer actually paid. The relevance of online ads, not surprisingly, relates to customers having previously searched for the desired product. (Mustri et al., 2023).

How do Amazon, Apple, and Facebook employ their enormous profits? In part, these monies enable substantial compensation packages for key personnel.

> The eye-popping compensation packages are just a sliver of the multibillion dollar investment the company is making to build the so-called metaverse, seemingly realistic computer-generated spaces in which users interact with one another. But Meta's high salaries and long-term investment in the metaverse also comes amid a frenzied push to rein in costs across the sprawling company.

(Nix, 2023)

Exploitation of Peers

There are almost two billion members of Facebook, Twitter, etc. They engage in various groups, viewing, posting, liking, retweeting, etc. Jonathan Haidt, a social psychologist, provides an insightful characterization of the overall phenomenon of social media (Haidt, 2019, 2022). He asserts that "human beings evolved to gossip, preen, manipulate, and ostracize." People are now more connected to one another on platforms that magnify these natural tendencies. These platforms, Haidt argues, have been designed to make outrage contagious.

Rose (2022) explores the phenomena of collective illusions. He argues, "Social media platforms allow anyone who's got an axe to grind to pull a digital power play, exerting direct control over the perceived majority and scaring all dissenters into silence with their unfiltered vehemence." He concludes, "Compromising your personal integrity for the sake of belonging quietly wears away at your self-esteem and has been shown to negatively affect personal health in both the short and the long term."

Consumers of misinformation and disinformation "have been manipulated to think that beliefs needn't change in response to evidence, making us more susceptible to conspiracy theories, science denial, and extremism" (Norman, 2021a). Norman makes a very compelling argument for fostering mental immunity (Norman, 2021b).

Education can provide the means to deter and mitigate misinformation and disinformation. As I later elaborate, it has been shown that students can learn how to detect, diagnose, and remediate false claims. There are compelling and viable proposals for how best to foster mental immunity to misinformation and disinformation (Norman, 2021b).

Klein (2020) explores polarization and identity politics. An increasing trend is for people to support candidates with whom they identify, regardless of their behaviors and policies. One dichotomy of importance is highly educated urban upper-middle-class people versus much less educated rural working-class people. In a nutshell, blue state versus red state citizens. These two populations increasingly distrust each other.

Medical Misinformation and Disinformation[1]

Misinformation and disinformation pose enormous public health risks (Rouse, Johns & Stead, 2022). Misleading advertisements, e.g., OxyContin, and misinformed or deceptive media pundits cause people to adopt practices to their detriment, or perhaps death. Such misinformation and disinformation are protected by free speech rights. Of course, people have long spread and believed in rumors and bought snake oil, health potions, and other shams, so the behavioral and social phenomena are not new. However, the connectivity and speed with which it now happens are unprecedented (Brossard & Scheufele, 2022).

Here are some examples of medical misinformation and disinformation:[1]

- Despite the lack of any evidence that various offerings can boost your immune system, and the possibility of negative side effects, the internet is filled with products that promise such a boost.
- A TV celebrity, an MD (medical doctor), touts unproven weight-loss pills and makes sweeping claims for Covid-19 cures despite minimal or non-existent evidence.
- The prenatal testing industry serves one-third of pregnant women in America, but tests have an 85% false alarm rate, higher for some rare diseases
- The pregnancy support app includes a section rife with scare stories, conspiracy theories, and outright falsehoods about the safety of vaccines, posted by app users.
- Seven out of eight newly approved drugs that do not provide previously unavailable benefits are promoted as if they do.
- The healthy are harmed due to providers' propensity to advocate what amounts to overdosing, over-treating, and over-diagnosing.

- The American Psychological Association reckons 10,000–20,000 mental-health apps are available for download. But evidence is mounting that privacy risks to users are being ignored. No one is checking if the apps work, either.
- Health insurance offerings that consumers do not realize may not, or will not, pay any claims for reimbursements.

The spectrum of purveyors and consumers of misinformation and disinformation ranges from people who are simply ignorant about science to a radical fringe element who use deliberate mistruths, intimidation, falsified data, and threats of violence in efforts to prevent the use of vaccines and to silence critics. Purveyors tend toward complete mistrust of government and manufacturers, conspiratorial thinking, denialism, low cognitive complexity in thinking patterns, reasoning flaws, and a habit of substituting emotional anecdotes for data.

Exploitation of Citizens

Internet and social media also create political and disruptive impacts on citizens, ranging from providing credence to posts and tweets, to sowing mistrust, to exploiting consumers' data, unbeknownst to these consumers.

Traditional Media

CNN, CNBC, Fox, and other traditional media companies have been greatly affected by social media. When breaking news includes statements like "As reported on Twitter…" you can see that these broadcasters are simply accepting tweets as true. This provides credence to assertions and announcements that have no basis of evidence.

Weaponization

Social media platforms also enable the "weaponization" via disinformation rather than misinformation (Singer & Brooking, 2018; Zegart, 2022). Adversaries, often via robots, sow mistrust in government and institutions. They attempt to affect elections via misinformation and disinformation. More broadly, they disrupt intelligence gathering and interpretation.

Cambridge Analytica

The *New York Times*, working with *The Observer* of London and *The Guardian*, obtained a cache of documents from inside Cambridge Analytica, the data firm principally owned by the right-wing donor Robert Mercer. The documents proved that the firm, where the former Trump aide Stephen Bannon was a board member, used data improperly obtained from Facebook to build voter profiles.

The *Times* reported that contractors and employees of Cambridge Analytica, eager to sell psychological profiles of American voters to political campaigns, acquired the private Facebook data of tens of millions of users – the largest known leak in Facebook history. The news put Cambridge under investigation and thrust Facebook into its biggest crisis ever.

(Confessore, 2018)

RESPONSES TO EXPLOITATION

An integrated response to mitigate exploitation is more likely to be enacted rather than piecemeal pieces of legislation having to overcome separate battles. Hence, I propose the following mitigation agenda.

Mitigation Agenda

In Chapter 4, I discussed several Department of Justice efforts to address monopolies. Despite having the laws and regulations they do not always win.

The U.S. Court of Appeals for the 9th Circuit agreed with a lower court's 2021 decision that Epic Games, the maker of Fortnite, failed to prove that Apple's App Store policies constituted anticompetitive conduct in violation of federal antitrust laws. The Court, however, upheld the lower court's ruling that Apple ran afoul of California competition laws because it forces developers to use Apple's payment processing service without allowing them to tell customers about cheaper alternatives.

(Zakrzewski, 2023)

As mentioned in Chapter 4, concerns about the clout and reach of Google, Facebook, Amazon, and Apple have grown. "Without the discipline of meaningful market-based competition, digital platforms may act in ways that are not responsive to consumer demands," observed the head of the Justice Department's antitrust division (Wakabayashi et al., 2019).

We need legislation regarding mechanisms to fight election interference. Intentionally deceiving qualified voters to prevent them from voting is voter suppression and is a federal crime. This legislation should require coordination with social media companies to flag the source of foreign political content (Posard et al., 2021).

We need to thwart misinformation and disinformation by funding the development of mechanisms for detection and remediation, perhaps by tagging, for example, assertions of medical impacts lacking evidence. As I elaborate in Chapter 6, we need to ban the advertising of prescription drugs on TV and radio. Many of these ads represent the art of misinformation.

We need to penalize misinformation and disinformation for the consequences of recipients acting on the information. Those who were convinced to avoid the coronavirus vaccines were 800% more likely to die if infected by the virus. Our cultural orientation is to let the buyer beware. We need mechanisms that, in effect, change the onus to let the liar beware.

Funding should be provided for information management education in K-12. It has been shown that young people can be trained to detect and reject misinformation and disinformation (Norman, 2021b; Rouse, Johns & Stead, 2022). It can easily be argued that such training amounts to a vaccine against misinformation and disinformation.

New Gilded Age

The concentration of wealth today rivals that of the Gilded Age. From 1860 to 1900, the wealthiest 10% of Americans owned roughly three-quarters of the nation's wealth. The bottom 40% had no wealth at all. Today, the top 10% of Americans still hold nearly 70% of US wealth, up from about 61% at the end of 1989. The bottom 50% own about 2.5% of the wealth.

Between 1979 and 2013, the top 1%'s share of income doubled nationally, increasing from 10% to 20%. Wealth concentration now exceeds that of the Gilded Age.

Will this precipitate a new Progressive Era? Any social media acts or technology anti-trust acts are likely to reflect such sentiments. However, these sentiments will have to be strongly embraced by the public to overcome Congressional inertia and the defense of the status quo. There is also the fortress of the First Amendment of the US Constitution (Rosenberg, 2021).

> Recent Supreme Court rulings did not definitively resolve the question of what responsibility platforms should have for the content posted on and recommended by their sites, an issue that has grown increasingly pressing as social media has become ubiquitous in modern life. But the decision by the court to pass for now on clarifying the breadth of Section 230, which dates to 1996, was cheered by the technology industry, which has long portrayed the law as integral to the development of the internet.
>
> **(Liptak, 2023)**

A recent Supreme Court ruling is rather alarming (Marimow & Barnes, 2023). The court

> reversed the conviction of a man who made extensive online threats to a stranger, saying free speech protections require prosecutors to prove the stalker was aware of the threatening nature of his communications. The state must show that the speaker intends the messages to be threatening.

The current court has demonstrated increasing tendencies to invoke the First Amendment to justify a growing range of rulings.

Thus, the mitigation agenda outlined above will need very strong grassroots support from the public, as well as Congressional support. This will likely have to be engendered bottom up. I consider how this can be enabled in Chapter 8.

Role of Government

The charters of the government agencies involved in the mitigation agenda are summarized in Table 5.2. Business practice issues are addressed by

TABLE 5.2

Selected US Government Agencies

Agency (Founding)	Agency Charter
DOJ (1870)	The United States Department of Justice, also known as the Justice Department, is a federal executive department of the United States government tasked with the enforcement of federal law and administration of justice in the United States. It is equivalent to the justice or interior ministries of other countries.
FCC (1934)	The Federal Communications Commission is an independent agency of the United States federal government that regulates communications by radio, television, wire, satellite, and cable across the United States.
FDA (1906)	The US Food and Drug Administration is responsible for protecting public health by ensuring the safety, efficacy, and security of human and veterinary drugs, biological products, medical devices, our nation's food supply, cosmetics, and products that emit radiation.
FTC (1914)	The Federal Trade Commission is an independent agency of the United States government whose principal mission is the enforcement of civil antitrust law and the promotion of consumer protection. The FTC shares jurisdiction over federal civil antitrust enforcement with the Department of Justice Antitrust Division.
SEC (1934)	The US Securities and Exchange Commission is an independent agency of the United States federal government, created in the aftermath of the Wall Street Crash of 1929. The primary purpose of the SEC is to enforce the law against market manipulation

the DOJ, FCC, FDA, FTC, and SEC, with the FDA playing a key role in medical misinformation and disinformation.

CONCLUSIONS

The financial and physical exploitations discussed in Chapters 3 and 4 are very tangible, measurable, and remediable, albeit with significant costs. The exploitations discussed in this chapter are primarily psychological, social, and political. We are only recently coming to understand the nature and impacts of such exploitations. It is not clear how best to mitigate polarization and regain trust.

Advertising revenues are driven by the frequency of likes and retweets. These are greater for outrageous content. As Haidt has argued, and I noted earlier, our cultural and social inclinations are to "gossip, preen, manipulate, and ostracize." A human-centered society has to foster and support mechanisms to mitigate these inclinations. This is central to health and wellness as I discuss in the next chapter.

NOTE

1 See Rouse, Johns and Stead (2022) for extensive references on the material in this section.

REFERENCES

Brossard, D., & Scheufele, D.A. (2022). The chronic growing pains of communicating science online. *Science*, 375 (6581), 613–614.

Bush, V. (1945). As we may think. *The Atlantic*, 176 (1), 101–108.

Confessore, N. (2018). Cambridge analytica and Facebook: The scandal and the fallout so far. The *New York Times*, April 4.

Haidt, J. (2022). Why the past 10 years of American life have been uniquely stupid: It's not just a phase. *The Atlantic*, April.

Haidt, J.R., & Rose-Stockwell, T. (2019). The dark psychology of social networks: Why it feels like everything has gone haywire. *The Atlantic*, December.

Isaacson, W. (2014). *The Innovators: How a Group of Hackers, Geniuses, and Geeks Created the Digital Revolution*. New York: Simon & Schuster.

Klein, E. (2020). *Why We Are Polarized*. New York: Simon & Schuster.

Licklider, J.C.R. (1960). Man-computer symbiosis. *IRE Transactions on Human Factors in Electronics*, Vol HFE-1, No 1, 4–11.

Licklider, J.C.R. (1965). *Libraries of the Future*. Cambridge, MA: MIT Press.

Liptak, A. (2023). Supreme Court won't hold tech companies liable for user posts. The *New York Times*, May 18.

Marimow, A.E., & Barnes, R. (2023). Supreme Court says a conviction for online threats violated 1st Amendment. *Washington Post*, June 27.

Mustri, E.A.S., Adjerid, I., & Acquisti, A. (2023). Behavioral advertising and consumer welfare: An empirical investigation. *Federal Trade Commission PrivacyCon 2022, Conference on Information Systems and Technology and Workshop on the Economics of Information Security*, November 1, 2022.

Nix, N. (2023). Salary packages approached $1 million as Meta paid to play in metaverse. *Washington Post*, April 7.

Norman, A. (2021a). The cause of America's post-truth predicament. *Scientific American*, May 18.

Norman, A. (2021b). *Mental Immunity: Infectious Ideas, Mind-Parasites, and the Search for a Better Way to Think*. New York: Harper.

Posard, M.N., Reininger, H., & Helmus, T.C. (2021). *Countering Foreign Interference in U.S. Elections*. Santa/Monica: RAND Corporation.

Rose, T. (2022). *Collective Illusions: Conformity, Complicity, and the Science of Why We Make Bad Decisions*. New York: Hachette.

Rosenberg, I. (2021). *The Fight for Free Speech: Ten Cases that Define Our First Amendment Freedoms*. New York: New York University Press.

Rouse, W.B., Johns, M.M.E, & Stead, W.W. (2022). *Medical Misinformation & Disinformation*. Washington, DC: McCourt School of Public Policy, Georgetown University.

Rouse, W.B., Lombardi, J.V., & Gargano, M. (2023). *Policy Innovations to Enhance the Stem Talent Pipeline: Interventions to Increase STEM Readiness of K-12 Students*. Hoboken, NJ: Systems Engineering Research Center, Stevens Institute of Technology.

Singer, P.W., & Brooking, E.T. (2018). *Like War: The Weaponization of Social Media*. Boston: Houghton Mifflin.

Tolk, A., Rouse, W.B., Pires, B.S., Cline, J.C, Diallo, S.Y., Sybil, A., & Russell, S.A. (2023). Applicability of artificial societies to evaluate health care policies. *Simulation in Healthcare*. https://doi.org/10.1097/SIH.0000000000000718.

Tyson, N.D. (2022). *Starry Messenger: Cosmic Perspectives on Civilization*. New York: Henry Holt.

Wakabayashi, D., Benner, K., & Lohr, S. (2019). Justice department opens antitrust review of big tech companies. *New York Times*, July 23.

Zakrzewski, C. (2023). Apple prevails in antitrust battle over the future of the App Store. *Washington Post*, April 24.

Zegart, A.B. (2022). *Spies, Lies & Algorithms: The History and Future of American Intelligence*. Princeton, NJ: Princeton University Press.

Zuboff, S. (2019). *The Age of Surveillance Capitalism: The Fight for a Human Future at the New Frontier of Power*. London: Profile Books.

6

Health and Wellness

Why does the US have the highest per capita expenditures among Organization for Economic Cooperation and Development (OECD) countries and the worst outcomes? Wolff and Aron (2023) report that

> Our life spans lag behind those of our peers; our life expectancy was already more or less flat, not growing; and most other countries bounced back from covid-19 in the second year of the pandemic, while we went into further decline.

Stein and colleagues (2022) suggest, however, that "global comparison can amount to nonsense due to obfuscation, misrepresentation, and omission of relevant information." Thus, there is some controversy on this issue.

Nevertheless, the US suffers from a fragmented non-system with little information sharing and care coordination. There are millions of entrepreneurs with no one in charge. These stakeholders are businesses trying to maximize profits and prevent encroachment on their stakes. They do not represent a human-centered social service. They are totally money-centered, not human-centered. In this chapter, I review how such exploitation happened and outline how we might mitigate such consequences.

INNOVATION IN HEALTH AND WELLNESS

It is important to differentiate innovations in medicine from innovations in healthcare delivery and payment. Innovations in medicine are, in general, beneficial to society in that they provide means to address health

DOI: 10.4324/9781003462361-6

and wellness challenges. In contrast, innovations in healthcare delivery and payment provide ample opportunities for exploitation and I discuss how stakeholders have leveraged these opportunities in great detail in this chapter.

Innovation – Medicine

I have listed below several well-known innovations in medicine. Space does not allow me to pursue this beyond the representatives noted below. Indeed, whole books have been devoted to this topic, e.g., (Engs, 2019).

- Louis Pasteur (1822–1895) identified principles of vaccination and pasteurization, Alexander Fleming (1881–1955) discovered penicillin in 1928
- Jonas Salk (1914–1995) created the first polio vaccine (inactivated poliovirus vaccine) in 1955, followed in 1960 by Albert Sabin's (1906–1993) oral polio vaccine
- Jerome Horwitz (1919–2012) created AZT in 1964 as a potential cancer drug; decades later AZT became the first successful drug treatment for people with AIDS
- Joseph Murray (1919–2012) and his team performed the first successful kidney transplant in 1954 with the recipient's identical twin as a donor; Christiaan Barnard (1922–2001) performed the world's first human-to-human heart transplant operation in 1967

Innovation – Healthcare Delivery

It should be kept in mind that our healthcare system emerged as it has over a long period of time, for a variety of reasons (Stevens, Rosenberg & Burns, 2006; Griffin, 2020; Push, 2022). In colonial times, rudimentary folk remedies were common. The Civil War resulted in enormous health challenges due to injuries and disease. Nevertheless, treatment was primarily fee-for-service, with payment due at the time of treatment.

From 1900 through 1965, the American Medical Association and other interests fiercely opposed government involvement in healthcare, arguing against socialized medicine, but actually focused on protecting physicians' independence and incomes. Nevertheless, government influence steadily grew. By the 1950s, and continuing today, healthcare costs were increasing far beyond inflation. One crisis seemed to follow another. I return to payment systems later in this section.

Integrated academic health centers began to emerge in the nineteenth century, including Massachusetts General Hospital (1811), Mayo Clinic (1889), Johns Hopkins School of Medicine (1893), and Cleveland Clinic (1921). Beyond treating patients, these centers provided medical education. Public hospitals also emerged, including Bellevue Hospital (1736), Charity Hospital (1736), and Grady Hospital (1896). Ross (2015) outlines their roles in serving people unable to pay for care.

Flexner Report

The American Medical Association formed the Council on Medical Education with the goal of restructuring American medical education. They contracted with the Carnegie Foundation for the Advancement of Teaching to survey American medical education. Carnegie chose Abraham Flexner to conduct the survey. Flexner was not a physician, a scientist, or a medical educator.

He visited every one of the 150 medical schools then in operation in North America. His findings were highly critical of contemporary education practices. Using Johns Hopkins as the model for quality medical education, he recommended reducing the number of medical schools, increasing the prerequisites to enter medical education, training physicians to practice in a scientific manner, engaging medical faculty in research, giving medical schools control of clinical instruction in hospitals, and strengthening state regulations of medical licensure (Flexner, 1910).

Many current aspects of the medical profession in North America are consequences of the Flexner Report. Many of its recommendations remain relevant – particularly those concerning the physician as a "social instrument whose function is fast becoming social and preventive, rather than individual and curative." This seminal report led to the science-based professionalization of medicine.

This initiative was not directly influenced by federal or state governments. However, it had enormous implications for governmental involvement in accreditation and licensing. In this way, the private sector led the public sector, but the support of the latter was essential to the eventual transformation of medicine.

Kaiser Permanente

My research into healthcare delivery has involved working with over ten major providers, involving several well-known thought leaders, many of whom are members of the National Academy of Medicine. I have, of course, experienced being a patient of several providers and being insured by several payers. I became a member of Kaiser Permanente (KP) in 2017 when I moved to Washington, DC. I encountered a complete outlier, very much a positive deviant in terms of accessibility and quality of service.

KP was founded in 1945 by industrialist Henry J. Kaiser and physician Sidney Garfield in Oakland, California. Operating in eight states and Washington, DC, it serves over 12 million members. KP operates 39 hospitals and more than 700 medical offices, with over 300,000 personnel, including more than 87,000 physicians and nurses. KP represents what population health should be (McKinsey, 2009; Pines et al., 2015). While KP only integrates limited educational and social services, it is easy to imagine their business model adapting to such needs.

KP closely coordinates primary, secondary, and hospital care, with a strong emphasis on prevention. They extensively use care pathways and electronic medical records. They carefully coordinate the work done by primary care physicians, specialists, hospitals, pharmacies, laboratories, and others. This improves care quality, makes care delivery more convenient for members, and increases communication among all the people providing care. It also enables them to find efficiencies that reduce costs, improve or maintain quality, and allow for innovation. KP's goal is to improve the overall health of the community, one person at a time (McKinsey, 2009).

KP is an integrated system consisting of three distinctly separate, but related entities: a health plan that bears insurance risk, medical groups of physicians, and a hospital system. The financial incentive is to provide high-quality, affordable care, and manage population health rather than generating a high volume of compensated services. Both the health plan and the medical group are aligned and accountable for a global budget, and only contract directly with one another for the provision of medical services. All three entities share the goal, reflected in the organization's capitated payment system, of keeping patients healthy while optimizing utilization (Pines et al., 2015)

How does a KP member experience this? As KP is the provider, payer, and pharmacy, I only need one relationship to cover my complete health needs. They are responsible for these needs within the capitated payments of Medicare Advantage, discussed below. Consequently, KP makes more profit when I am healthy. They do their best to keep me healthy with emails, surveys, e.g., on mental health, and other forms of outreach. Other than my monthly Medicare deduction from my Social Security benefit, I spend very little on healthcare.

I see population health initiatives eventually resulting in Medicare Advantage for everyone as provided by KP. I imagine there will be multiple private sector participants in this integrated system, some of them profit-making. However, as a member, I will not have to know about any of the pieces. I will just experience high-quality, affordable, and fully understandable care.

Telemedicine

The Institute of Medicine, now the National Academy of Medicine, defined telemedicine in 1996 as "the use of electronic information and communications technologies to provide and support healthcare when distance separates participants" (NAP, 2012). A wide range of telemedicine practices has been in use for many decades.

A primary impediment to adoption has been reimbursement practices that limit payments to face-to-face visits at clinicians' offices, clinics, and hospitals. Another impediment has been state licensing laws that limit clinicians' abilities to practice across state lines. Thus, technological capabilities and effectiveness have not been significant hurdles.

The first break in this deadlock occurred relatively recently. In 2018, the US Department of Veterans Affairs (VA) announced: "a new federal rule that will allow VA doctors, nurses and other healthcare providers to administer care to Veterans using telehealth, or virtual technology, regardless of where in the United States the provider or Veteran is located" (VA, 2018).

The coronavirus pandemic of 2020 has, at least temporarily, eliminated the impediments (CMS, 2020). The use of telemedicine for outpatient care has grown from 1% to roughly 70%. Estimates of increased usage have ranged from 11,000% to 20,000% (Licurse et al., 2020). Such extremes are unlikely to be sustained after the pandemic. However, necessity has been the mother of invention and this innovation will likely be sustained, particularly for providers who are also payers, e.g., Kaiser Permanente and Veterans Health.

Summary

In this section, I have outlined several innovations in the delivery of care that, over time, leverage the innovations in medicine discussed earlier. Next, I address innovations in payment systems. Innovations in medicine and delivery tend to cut across geography and politics globally. Payment, however, is different in that the US is the only OECD country that does not provide government-paid universal coverage. This is an enormous factor in the types of exploitation discussed later in this chapter.

Innovations – Payment Systems

The first instance of health insurance as we now know it came at Baylor in 1929 (BCBS, 2023). This forerunner of Blue Cross began as a partnership between a local hospital and its financially struggling patients. Baylor University hospital administrators sought a way to make healthcare more affordable for their patients, many of whom were Dallas public school teachers. Blue Cross merged with Blue Shield to form the Blue Cross and Blue Shield Association in 1982. The Association currently has 115 million members.

Social Security

The New Deal was a series of programs initiated during the Great Depression by President Franklin D. Roosevelt with the goal of restoring prosperity to Americans. When Roosevelt took office in 1933, he acted swiftly to stabilize the economy and provide jobs and relief to people who were suffering the economic consequences of the Depression.

The New Deal's social welfare programs included the Resettlement Administration (RA), the Rural Electrification Administration (REA), rural welfare projects sponsored by the Works Progress Administration (WPA), National Youth Administration (NYA), Forest Service, and the Civilian Conservation Corps (CCC). The centerpiece of the New Deal was the Social Security Act that Roosevelt signed into law on August 14, 1935.

The act created a social insurance program that paid retired workers age 65 or older a continuing income after retirement.

A primary goal of Social Security was to protect aged and disabled people from the expenses of illnesses that might deplete their savings. One of the motivations for the act was a tendency for elderly people to avoid medical care that they felt they could not afford. Social Security expenditures have grown to roughly 25% of the federal budget.

Employer-Based Insurance

The Stabilization Act of 1942 limited wage increases, hoping to stem inflation during World War II. In reaction to protests, the War Labor Board exempted employer-paid health benefits from wage controls and income tax in 1943. The saga of employer-based health insurance began in 1945 (Smith, 2021).

Corporate greed and profiteering, higher utilization of costly medical technology, and steadily increasing administrative expenses have driven healthcare costs since then.

> By the 2000s, the employer-provided health insurance death spiral had begun to run its course. From 1999 to 2020, without accounting for the annual benefit reductions, the cost to cover a single employee rose from $2,196 per year to $7,470 per year. Family coverage increased from $5,791 per year in 1999 to $21,342 per year in 2020.
>
> **(Smith, 2021)**

Over the past several decades in the US, wages have stagnated at an annual growth rate of 1–2%, particularly for low-wage workers. At the same, the costs of labor to employers have grown annually by 8–10%. This difference is due to the steadily increasing costs of health insurance. Healthcare providers charge patients with employer-based insurance roughly twice what they charge Medicare and Medicaid patients. They make up their losses on these patients by overcharging others.

Case and Deaton (2020) report that median wages for white working-class men have been declining for four decades. Their total earnings have declined by 21% while their total compensation, including benefits, has risen by 68%. This amazing difference is attributable to the costs of employer-based health insurance.

Put simply, people are sacrificing wage increases to pay health insurance increases to compensate for other people's healthcare costs. Employee co-pays have increased, but people still like their "free" insurance. However, it is far from free as they have sacrificed possible substantial raises to this "hidden tax." People are unknowingly subsidizing patients for which the government will not pay the full costs of healthcare. The government has masked this exploitation of wage earners.

In the early 1990s, the software company that I led had roughly 40 employees and 100 covered lives. Our annual healthcare costs doubled in one year due to a newborn child having difficulties in the early months, that were eventually overcome. This is a compelling example of a health insurance company passing its risks to patients.

Medicare and Medicaid

Roosevelt tried to include national health insurance in the Social Security Act of 1935 but could not bring together enough support. The American Medical Association (AMA) attacked the idea. The National Health Care Acts of 1939 and 1943 failed as well.

President Harry Truman included universal healthcare in his Fair Deal in 1945 and 1949 but strong opposition stopped it. The AMA, the American Hospital Association, the American Bar Association, and most of the nation's press detested the plan, labeling it as "socialized medicine," which was associated with the idea of communism.

By the 1960s, public opinion had shifted towards the problem of the uninsured, especially the elderly. This, of course, would likely affect everyone eventually. According to the Department of Health, Education, and Welfare, the problem of elderly Americans lacking healthcare was substantial. Older Americans required much more hospital care than younger people. Social Security benefits were not sufficient to cover the costs of hospitalization, which were already rising rapidly due to medical advances.

Senator John Kennedy announced his support for what was now called Medicare during his 1960 Presidential campaign. As President, Kennedy authorized a substantial public-relations effort in support of Medicare. The AMA launched an aggressive campaign in opposition to this initiative. The insurance lobby worked in the background to undermine the bill.

Democratic Representative Wilbur Mills of Arkansas, chair of the House Ways and Means Committee, stood in the way of the legislation. Kennedy sent the proposal to Congress, but Mills would not bring the Medicare bill up for a vote.

When Lyndon Johnson became President, he was determined to pass Medicare. His overriding goal was to pass a second New Deal. Medicare was at the top of his list, as well as civil rights. With the 1964 landslide election, the Democrats controlled everything. Outnumbered, Mills had no choice but to go along.

In crafting the legislation, Mills argued for adding what would become Medicaid. He was also creative in defining how the costs of Medicare and Medicaid would be paid. President Lyndon Johnson signed the Social Security Amendments of 1965 into law on July 30, 1965. These programs now consume 25% of the federal budget.

A range of modifications and extensions of Medicare and Medicaid have been legislated since their inception. The Health Insurance Portability and Accountability Act (HIPAA) was enacted in 1996. This Federal law requires the creation of national standards to protect sensitive patient health information from being disclosed without the patient's consent or knowledge.

It was soon followed by the Children's Health Insurance Program (CHIP) in 1997. This program provides health coverage to eligible children, through both Medicaid and separate CHIP programs. CHIP is administered by states, according to federal requirements. The program is funded jointly by states and the federal government.

The Medicare Prescription Drug, Improvement, and Modernization Act of 2003 provided two important extensions. Medicare Advantage established a capitated program for providing Medicare benefits in the United States. Under Part C, Medicare pays a private sector health insurer a fixed payment. The insurer then pays for the healthcare expenses of enrollees. I am a proponent of this as mentioned earlier. Almost half of Medicare recipients have enrolled in Medicare Advantage.

The second extension was Medicare Part D, which helps cover the cost of prescription drugs. Part D is optional, but offered to everyone who qualifies for Medicare, and is only provided through private insurance companies approved by the federal government. Costs and coverage tend to vary from plan to plan.

Affordable Care Act

The Affordable Care Act (ACA), formally known as the Patient Protection and Affordable Care Act, and commonly known as Obamacare, was enacted by the United States Congress and signed into law by President Barack Obama on March 23, 2010. The bill passed in the House by 220 to 215 and in the Senate by 60 to 40. Only one Republican in the House and none in the Senate voted for the bill. The lone Republican vote came after the vote total was already sufficient to pass the bill.

The act largely retained the existing structure of Medicare, Medicaid, and the employer market, but individual markets were substantially changed. Insurers had to accept all applicants and prices could not be based on pre-existing conditions or demographic status, other than age. To combat the problem of low-risk patients avoiding buying insurance, it was mandated that individuals buy insurance or pay a fine and that insurers cover a list of "essential health benefits."

The case for change was compelling. There were 50 million people without healthcare coverage. There was evidence that the healthcare system was not always delivering at the highest quality. For example, if you had diabetes, you only got recommended care about half of the time. It was very difficult to get such major legislation passed through the House and Senate and signed by the President, particularly because this legislation was complicated and had vast impacts. Fortunately, the example of Massachusetts showed that it could be done. Nevertheless, presidential leadership was absolutely critical (Seervai, 2020).

This is an excellent example of innovation in a complex public-private ecosystem. Key stakeholders included the public, of course, but also providers, payers, and suppliers of drugs and devices. The "story" had to explain how this would work for everyone, what compromises were necessary, and how it would be economically feasible. Nevertheless, many Members of Congress opposed the bill.

21st Century Cures Act

This United States law was enacted in 2016. Provisions benefit patients, healthcare providers, and health IT developers. For example, improved interoperability and the prevention of information blocking related to the access, exchange, or use of electronic health records. It also ensures healthcare providers are compliant with new mandates.

Integrative Assessments

Over the past decade or so, we conducted various assessments of the state of healthcare delivery in the US. Denis Cortese, then CEO of Mayo Clinic, and I recruited a wide range of thought leaders to provide perspectives on how to best engineer the system of healthcare delivery (Rouse & Cortese, 2010). That same year, we compiled expert perspectives on economic valuation on investments in people's training and education, health and safety, and work productivity (Rouse, 2010).

A few years later, Nicoleta Serban and I focused on understanding and managing the complexity of healthcare (Rouse & Serban, 2014). We addressed the ways in which healthcare delivery is complex, how to computationally represent this complexity, and address possible mitigations. Most recently, I mapped out strategies for transforming the health ecosystem (Rouse, 2022). We know how to dramatically improve effectiveness and efficiency. It will require that we address the stewards of the status quo who are exploiting the current ecosystem.

EXPLOITATION IN HEALTH AND WELLNESS

Table 6.1 briefly summarizes forms of innovation and exploitation in health and wellness. We need to creatively balance business innovation and social exploitation to foster a human-centered society. This will require reigning in exploitation. Primary exploiters include providers, payers, and pharma companies that prioritize profits over human needs (Lancet, 2023). These trends are increasingly alienating physicians (Press, 2023).

TABLE 6.1

Innovation and Exploitation in Health and Wellness

Innovations	Public health, vaccines, genomics, and telehealth.
Financial exploitation	Monopoly pricing, depressed wages, waste, fraud, and abuse.
Physical exploitation	Avoidable disease, failed treatment, and early death.
Psychological exploitation	False advertising, misinformation, and disinformation.
Mitigating exploitation	Regulations, anti-trust laws, advertising laws, and externality taxes.

Exploitation by Providers and Payers

From a business perspective, healthcare providers want to charge as much as possible while healthcare insurers want to pay as little as possible. The fee-for-service payment system encourages the maximization of services delivered. Payers counter this by requiring approval for services, particularly expensive services.

As discussed earlier, providers overcharge patients with employer-based insurance, arguing that this is required due to marginal Medicare reimbursements and inadequate Medicaid reimbursements. I elaborated on the very negative consequences of this practice on employee earnings. However, our fragmented system has difficulty addressing this.

Prevention is very poorly reimbursed, if at all. This is less the case for Medicare Advantage as providers and payers are incentivized to manage their capitated payments to yield profits. Kaiser Permanente is well-positioned to manage both sides of this equation.

The consequences of all of the above are high costs and poor outcomes. Of course, these costs translate into revenue and profits for both providers and payers. Such business opportunities are exploited to maximize profits and deter competition. Enormous vested interests will do their best to thwart efforts to change the rules of the game.

Exploitation by Pharma

John Abramson (2022) reports in his recent book *Sickening* how big pharma broke American healthcare and how we can repair it. He explains how pharmaceutical companies have avoided evidence-based reporting and contributed to the US being first in healthcare spending and 68th in healthcare outcomes. We are spending enormous amounts on things that do not work.

Why is this happening? Advertising of prescription drugs, i.e., the endless ads of happy people, supposedly due to their consuming one prescription or another, only happens in the US and New Zealand. The pharma companies do not disclose their evidence of the efficacy of their offerings to the FDA because of "proprietary interests." The FDA just takes the word of these companies.

What can we do to overcome such practices? First of all, the evidence of the efficacy of a healthcare intervention should not be provided by those trying to sell you the intervention. Second, there needs to be standards of evidence, and social media rarely, if ever, meet such standards. Third, the purveyors of misinformation and disinformation need to be liable for the consequences of people believing them. The eventual enormous consequences to Purdue Pharma for the OxyContin epidemic were very slow in coming, but at least happened.

Patent Manipulation

Feldman (2018) and Nawrat (2019) report on patent manipulation by pharma companies. Two common manipulations are termed "thicketing" and "evergreening." A patent thicket is "an overlapping set of patent rights" that requires innovators to reach licensing deals for multiple patents.

Evergreening is any of various legal, business, and technological strategies by which pharmaceutical companies extend the lifetime of their patents that are about to expire in order to retain revenues from them. This involves making small changes to branded drugs – such as through modes of administration, new dosages, and even simply the color of the drug itself – which sometimes do not confer more therapeutic benefit to the patients.

A total of 78% of drugs associated with new patents are not new drugs, but existing ones, and almost 40% of all drugs on the market had additional market barriers through further exclusivities. More than 70% of the 100 best-selling drugs between 2005 and 2015 had their protection extended at least once, with almost 50% receiving more than one exclusivity extension.

Prescription Pricing

Prescription drugs cost 250% as much in the US as they do in other countries. Yet the pharma companies report very low taxable profits.

> They assign patents and other forms of intellectual property to overseas subsidiaries located in low-tax jurisdictions. Their US operations then pay large fees to these overseas subsidiaries for the use of this intellectual property, magically causing profits to disappear here and reappear someplace else, where they go largely untaxed.

(Krugman, 2023)

Pharma exploitation is intended to maximize profits and deter competitors, as exemplified by Merck's resistance to price negotiations (Roubein & Beard, 2023). Bristol Myers Squibb joined the chorus of pharma companies trying to preserve enormous profit margins by avoiding negotiations (Tan, 2023).

The pharma business model encourages dependencies, not cures. Advertising encourages such dependencies. An exemplar is Purdue Pharma's false advertisements and marketing promotions of OxyContin, precipitating over one million deaths.

> Nearly 200 people signed a letter strongly criticizing pharmaceutical companies for putting a desire to make extraordinary profits before the needs of humanity. Selling publicly funded vaccines, treatments, and tests to the highest bidder resulted in inequities that cost more than a million lives, while private companies made billions of dollars.
>
> **(Lancet, 2023)**

Summary

> Commercial actors can contribute positively to health and society, and many do, providing essential products and services. However, a substantial group of commercial actors are escalating avoidable levels of ill health, planetary damage, and inequity – the commercial determinants of health. While policy solutions are available, they are not currently being implemented, and the costs of harm caused by some products and practices are coming at a great cost to individuals and society.
>
> **(Lancet, 2023)**

RESPONSES TO EXPLOITATION

An integrated response to mitigate exploitation is more likely to be enacted rather than piecemeal pieces of legislation having to overcome separate battles. Hence, I propose the following mitigation agenda.

Mitigation Agenda

Legislation will be needed to address several issues. Providers should be banned from charging higher prices to employer-based payers. Centers for Medicare & Medicaid Services (CMS) could facilitate this by denying access to Medicare patients by any providers violating this condition. This will require a unified and transparent payment system in the US. It will be immediately apparent if payers, and hence employers, are being exploited.

To enable this change, Medicare and Medicaid reimbursement rates will have to increase. This will be balanced by significant decreases in administrative costs due to the unified and transparent payment system. Lower costs to employers will enable salary and wage increases, which will increase income tax revenues.

Medicare should be enabled to negotiate prescription drug prices with pharma companies. CMS and the Food & Drug Administration (FDA) will play a role in this, as the FDA will need to certify the efficacy of drugs based on data openly provided by the pharma companies. The lack of such data will preclude companies from selling their drugs in the US.

Prescription drug ads should be banned on television and radio. The Federal Communications Commission (FCC) and FDA will play roles in this. "Public service" pieces that attempt to circumvent this regulation will be subject to indictments in the federal criminal justice system. Pharma companies will, of course, be able to distribute marketing materials directly to providers.

US patent protections should be limited to prevent thicketing and evergreening. This will be overseen by the USPTO and the FDA. Applications to extend patents will be required to provide verifiable evidence that extensions provide significantly enhanced patient benefits, e.g., changing the color of the drug will fail this requirement.

As noted above, a unified, transparent payment system will be needed to enforce this agenda. This might be an element of an overall effort by the National Library of Medicine to assure the validity of health-related information in support of decision-making by providers, payers, pharm, and especially consumers.

US Health Board

If the US finance and banking ecosystem operated like the healthcare ecosystem, the resulting fragmentation would completely undermine the system, e.g., perhaps each state would have its own currency. Fortunately the Federal Reserve Board assures sharing of information and coordination of services. With this end in mind, the Blue Ridge Academic Health Group has recommended the following nationwide policy framework (BRAHG, 2008) to underlie a US Health Board that will:

- Bring together leaders from across the healthcare spectrum in a private-public organizational structure conducive to long-term planning and decision-making (to bring stability and consistency to a system now buffeted about from one election cycle to the next)
- Take up the key challenges facing our healthcare system such as health insurance benefit equity, attention to mission-critical and vulnerable populations, insurance reform and pooling risk; and economic viability (to embark on a course of needed change that allows system participants to make long-term investments and patients to adapt with changes to lifestyle behaviors because there is a longer-term planning horizon for system configuration)
- Standardize and simplify the capture of health information and financial data, including encounter forms and billing transactions among the government, private insurers and providers of healthcare services (to eliminate waste)
- Collect and analyze encounter-level data specific to individual providers so as to enable identification of best practices and the most effective models for health services delivery (to reduce variation)
- Make information available to the public and to the healthcare community (to inform healthcare decision-making)

A very recent proposal by Byyny (2023) argues for a similar mechanism, in this case called a National Health Reserve System, patterned after the Federal Reserve.

Role of Government

The charters of the government agencies involved in the mitigation agenda are summarized in Table 6.2. A few agencies not discussed above are included due to their particular relevance to health and wellness.

Motivating Change

All of the stakeholders in the health ecosystem have premised their business models on the assumption that the economic system will continue to

TABLE 6.2

Selected US Government Agencies

Agency (Founding)	Agency Charter
CDC (1946)	The Centers for Disease Control and Prevention is the national public health agency of the United States. It is a United States federal agency under the Department of Health and Human Services, whose main goal is the protection of public health and safety through the control and prevention of disease, injury, and disability in the US and worldwide.
CMS (1965)	The Centers for Medicare and Medicaid Services is a federal agency within the United States Department of Health and Human Services that administers the Medicare program and works in partnership with state governments to administer Medicaid, the Children's Health Insurance Program (CHIP), and health insurance portability standards.
FCC (1934)	The Federal Communications Commission is an independent agency of the United States federal government that regulates communications by radio, television, wire, satellite, and cable across the United States.
FDA (1906)	The US Food and Drug Administration is responsible for protecting public health by ensuring the safety, efficacy, and security of human and veterinary drugs, biological products, medical devices, our nation's food supply, cosmetics, and products that emit radiation.
NIOSH (1970)	The National Institute for Occupational Safety and Health is the United States federal agency responsible for conducting research and making recommendations for the prevention of work-related injury and illness.
OSHA (1971)	The Occupational Safety and Health Administration is a large regulatory agency of the United States Department of Labor that originally had federal visitorial powers to inspect and examine workplaces, whose workplace safety inspections have been shown to reduce injury rates and injury costs without adverse effects on employment, sales, credit ratings, or firm survival.
SAMSHA (1992)	The Substance Abuse and Mental Health Services Administration is a branch of the US Department of Health and Human Services charged with improving the quality and availability of treatment and rehabilitative services in order to reduce illness, death, disability, and the cost to society resulting from substance abuse and mental illnesses.
USPTO (1836)	The United States Patent and Trademark Office is an agency in the US Department of Commerce that serves as the national patent office and trademark registration authority for the United States.

operate as it has been since they made these commitments. These business models will only be changed if these stakeholders have no choice. We need a "burning platform" to motivate the needed changes.

I suggest that two changes in the incentive system will create this burning platform. First, providers of care, as well as equipment, devices, and supplies, should be paid for outcomes in terms of improved health and decreased risks of disease. They should not be paid for the costs of their procedures or the number of procedures conducted. Their payment should be linked to the extent to which a patient is better off than they would have been without the providers' services. Ideally, we would create market mechanisms that would enable and motivate people to determine the extent to which they are better off, and then pay accordingly.

Second, as noted above, it should be illegal for providers to charge patients with employer-based insurance more than they are allowed to charge Medicare and Medicaid patients. If such "cost shifting" was illegal, the system would have to change because either all providers would soon go out of business or Medicare and Medicaid patients would not receive any care. The invisible tax embodied in cost shifting has significantly depressed wage levels across the US for the past two decades. Making this practice visible – and then illegal – would force change.

One might argue that these two suggestions would result in poor and elderly people receiving inadequate care. However, the opposite would happen. If one is only paid for improving people's health, then one needs to find lots of unhealthy and at-risk people. That is where improvements can be achieved and money made. Focusing on healthy, low-risk people would be a poor choice as one cannot improve their health sufficiently to stay in business.

CONCLUSIONS

Health and wellness have benefitted and will continue to benefit from the efforts of well-intended and committed people and organizations. The caring side of the health ecosystem is strong and to be admired.

The business side of the ecosystem is suspect. It prioritizes maximizing revenues and profits while minimizing costs.

A degree of this orientation is admittedly necessary to stay in business. However, current levels of exploitation are clearly excessive. Here is one indicator. According to Becker (2023), "Pharmaceutical and health insurance CEOs are among the highest-paid executives of the largest U.S. companies."

A human-centered society aspires to have a healthy, educated, and productive population that is competitive in the global marketplace. Aggressive exploitation is incompatible with this objective. However, exploitation is a natural tendency among many people. Consequently, we need to understand the hallmarks of exploitation and have mechanisms that can moderate such aspirations.

REFERENCES

Abramson, J. (2022). *Sickening: How Big Pharma Broke American Health Care and How We Can Repair It*. Boston: Mariner.

BCBS. (2023). *Blue Cross: Origins*. https://www.bcbs.com/about-us/industry-pioneer. Accessed 06/08/23.

Becker. (2023). 11 highest paid CEOs in healthcare. *Becker Hospital Review*, May 15.

BRAHG. (2008). *A United States Health Board*. Atlanta, GA: Blue Ridge Academic Health Group.

Byyny, R. (2023). Good isn't good enough: Why the United States should develop a new NHRS system of health care delivery. Pharos, Spring.

Case, A., & Deaton, A. (2020) *Deaths of Despair*. Princeton, NJ: Princeton University Press.

CMS. (2020). *Trump Administration Drives Telehealth in Medicare and Medicaid*. Baltimore, MD: Centers for Medicare & Medicaid Services Press Release, October 14.

Engs, R.C. (Ed.). (2019). *Health and Medicine Through History: From Ancient Practices to 21st-Century Innovations*. Santa Barbara, CA: Greenwood.

Feldman, R. (2018). May your drug prices be evergreen. *Journal of Law and the Biosciences*, 590–647. https://doi.org/10.1093/jlb/lsy022.

Flexner, A. (1910). *Medical Education in the United States and Canada: A Report to the Carnegie Foundation for the Advancement of Teaching*. New York City: The Carnegie Foundation for the Advancement of Teaching, Bulletin No. 4.

Galea, S. (2019). *Well: What We Need to Talk About When We Talk About Health*. Oxford: Oxford University Press.

Griffin, J. (2020). The history of medicine and organized healthcare in America. *HUB*, March 27.

Ho, C.J., Skead, H.K.K., & Wong, J. (2022). The politics of universal health coverage. *Lancet*, 399, 2066–2074.

Hoffman, B. (2003). Health care reform and social movements in the United States. *American Journal of Public Health*, 93 (1), 75–85.

Insel, T. (2022). *Healing: Our Path from Mental Illness to Mental Health.* New York: Penguin.

Krugman, P. (2023). Attack of the pharma phantoms. *New York Times*, May 12.

Lancet. (2023). Unravelling the commercial determinants of health. *Lancet*, 401, April 8.

Licurse, A., Fanning, K., Laskowski, K., & Nadman, A. (2020). Balancing virtual and in-person health care. *Harvard Business Review*, November 17.

Marmot, M. (2016). *The Health Gap: Improving Health in an Unequal World.* London: Bloomsbury.

McKinsey. (2009). What health systems can learn from Kaiser Permanente – An interview with Hal Wolf. *McKinsey Quarterly*, July 1.

NAP. (2012). *Telehealth in an Evolving Healthcare Environment.* Washington, DC: National Academies Press.

Nawrat, A. (2019). From evergreening to thicketing: Exploring the manipulation of pharma patents. *Pharmaceutical Technology.com*. https://www.pharmaceutical-technology.com/features/pharma-patents-manpulation/. Accessed 06/08/23.

Pines, J., Selevan, J., McStay, F., George, M., & McClellan, M. (2015). *Kaiser Permanente – California: A Model for Integrated Care for the Ill and Injured.* Washington, DC: Brookings Institution, Center for Health Policy.

Press, E. (2023). The moral crisis of America's doctors: The corporatization of health care has changed the practice of medicine, causing many physicians to feel alienated from their work. *New York Times Magazine*, June 15.

Push, A. (2022). A brief look at American health care's long, complicated history. *Sidecar Health.* https://sidecarhealth.com/blog/a-brief-look-at-american-health-cares-long-complicated-history/.

Ross, W. (2015). *Urban Health and the History of Public Hospitals in the US.* St. Louis, MO: Washington University School of Medicine.

Roubein, R., & Beard, M. (2023). How Merck intends to fight Medicare drug price negotiation. *Washington Post*, June 7.

Rouse, W.B. (Ed.). (2010). *The Economics of Human Systems Integration: Valuation of Investments in People's Training and Education, Safety and Health, and Work Productivity.* New York: John Wiley.

Rouse, W.B. (2022). *Transforming Public-Private Ecosystems: Understanding and Enabling Innovation in Complex Systems.* Oxford: Oxford University Press.

Rouse, W.B., & Cortese, D.A. (Eds.). (2010). *Engineering the System of Healthcare Delivery.* Amsterdam: IOS Press.

Rouse, W.B., & Serban, N. (2014). *Understanding and Managing the Complexity of Healthcare.* Cambridge, MA: MIT Press.

Seervai, S. (2020). *A Monumental Effort: How Obamacare Was Passed – An Interview with Liz Fowler.* New York: The Commonwealth Fund, March 20.

Smith, G. (2021). The complete history of employer-provided health insurance. *People Keep.* Accessed 06/07/23.

Stein, F., Storeng, K.T., & Puyvallée, A.D. (2022). Global health nonsense. *BMJ*, 379. https://doi.org/10.1136/bmj.o2932.

Stevens, R.A., Rosenberg, C.E., & Burns, L.R. (Eds.). (2006). *History & Health Policy in the United States*. New Brunswick, NJ: Rutgers University Press.

Tan, E. (2023). Eliquis maker Bristol Myers Squibb sues over medicare plan to cut drug costs. *Washington Post*, June 16.

VA. (2018). *VA Expands Telehealth by Allowing Health Care Providers to Treat Patients Across State Lines*. https://www.va.gov/opa/pressrel/pressrelease.cfm?id=4054.

Wolff, S.H., & Aron, L. (2023). American life expectancy is dropping – And it's not all covid's fault. *Washington Post*, June 1.

7

Energy and Climate

In Chapter 3, we were buying cars. Chapter 4 saw us buying laptops and digital devices. In Chapter 5, we consumed the Internet and social media. Chapter 6 addressed services for health and well-being. All of these ecosystems consume energy. We cannot meaningfully address the challenges in these ecosystems without considering the energy sources involved and the environmental consequences.

In this chapter, I focus directly on innovations in energy extraction, conversion, and transmission, as well as innovations in oversight of the industry. I then address the financial, physical, and psychological exploitation that has followed these innovations. As in the earlier chapters, I adopt a human-centered perspective on how best to mitigate such exploitation.

INNOVATIONS IN ENERGY AND CLIMATE

People have long taken advantage of water, wind, and wood power. As discussed in Chapter 2, the wood economy in New England was the beginning of the US energy industry. The evolution of the energy industry is chronicled by Grubler (2012), Newell (2011), and Power (2022). The future of the industry is likely to continue creating many innovations, for example advanced nuclear power (NAP, 2023) and hydrogen-based power plants (Puko, 2023).

To summarize industry innovations, it is useful to distinguish extraction, conversion, and transmission, each of which has its own challenges:

  DOI: 10.4324/9781003462361-7

- Extraction: The goal is less expensive extraction
- Conversion: The goal is more efficient conversion
- Transmission: The goal is more efficient transmission

Innovations in Extraction

In 1853, Samuel Kier established America's first commercial oil refinery on Seventh Avenue, near Grant Street in Pittsburgh, Pennsylvania. He used crude oil from salt wells. Edwin Drake was the first person to strike oil in America. His world-famous well was drilled in Titusville, Pennsylvania, a small town in Crawford County, in 1859.

Photovoltaic technology was born in the United States in 1954 when Daryl Chapin, Calvin Fuller, and Gerald Pearson developed the silicon photovoltaic (PV) cell at Bell Labs. It was the first solar cell capable of converting enough of the sun's energy into power to run electrical equipment.

George P. Mitchell has been called the "father of fracking" because of his role in applying it in shales. The first horizontal well in the Barnett Shale was drilled in 1991, but was not widely done in the Barnett until it was demonstrated that gas could be economically extracted from vertical wells in the Barnett.

Innovations in Conversion

People used wind energy to propel boats along the Nile River as early as 5000 BCE. By 200 BC, simple wind-powered water pumps were used in China, and windmills with woven-reed blades were grinding grain in Persia and other parts of the Middle East. The Dutch were building windmills as early as 1200 AD to use them for grinding grains. There were more than 9,000 windmills in Holland by the nineteenth century.

James Watt (1736–1819) was a Scottish instrument maker and inventor whose steam engine in 1769 contributed substantially to the Industrial Revolution. Robert Fulton designed and operated the world's first commercially successful steamboat, based on Watt's engine. His Clermont made its first run in 1807 on the Hudson River.

By 1827, Czech-Austrian inventor Josef Ressel had invented a screw propeller with multiple blades on a conical base. He tested it in February

1826 on a manually driven ship and successfully used it on a steamboat in 1829. By the twentieth-century, propellers were pervasive on airplanes.

In 1849, British-American engineer James Francis developed the first modern water turbine which remains the most widely used water turbine in the world today. The world's first hydroelectric power plant began operation on the Fox River in Appleton, Wisconsin, in 1882. The plant was initiated by Appleton paper manufacturer H.J. Rogers, who had been inspired by Thomas Edison's plans for an electricity-producing station in New York.

Nicolaus August Otto (1832–1891) was a German engineer who successfully developed the compressed charge internal combustion engine in 1876 which ran on petroleum gas and led to the modern internal combustion engine. Karl Benz focused on creating a dependable vehicle inspired by Nikolaus Otto's engine innovations.

American rocketry pioneer Robert H. Goddard demonstrated his first liquid-fueled rocket in 1926 using gasoline as fuel and liquid oxygen as an oxidizer. Such rockets were critical to enabling space exploration as guidance and control required dependable sources of power.

Frank Whittle formally submitted his ideas for a turbo-jet to his superiors in 1928. Whittle submitted his first patent application in 1930, which was granted in 1932. The patent showed a two-stage axial compressor feeding a single-sided centrifugal compressor. Practical axial compressors were made possible by ideas from A.A. Griffith in a seminal paper in 1926. Whittle had his first engine running in April 1937.

The Shippingport Atomic Power Station in Shippingport, Pennsylvania, the first full-scale nuclear power generating station in the United States, began operating in 1957, serving as the world's first scalable nuclear power plant. The United States had 93 operating commercial nuclear reactors at 55 nuclear power plants in 28 states at the end of 2021.

Innovations in Transmission

Edison championed direct current (DC) as the prevailing method for electrical distribution, while Tesla saw the potential of alternating current (AC) systems, which offered greater efficiency over longer distances. The AC power system was developed and adopted rapidly after 1886 due to its ability to distribute electricity efficiently over long distances, overcoming the limitations of the direct current system.

- 1882 – The first distribution systems were built by Edison in Manhattan and New Jersey. These systems use direct current over copper wiring.
- 1896 – The first alternating current line was built to connect Niagara Falls to Buffalo, New York.
- 1907 – Commonwealth Edison became the first to consolidate power companies into one unit.

The first official definition of Smart Grid was provided by the Energy Independence and Security Act of 2007. Title XIII of this bill provides a description, with ten characteristics, that can be considered a definition for Smart Grid, as follows:

(1) Increased use of digital information and controls technology to improve reliability, security, and efficiency of the electric grid.
(2) Dynamic optimization of grid operations and resources, with full cyber-security.
(3) Deployment and integration of distributed resources and generation, including renewable resources.
(4) Development and incorporation of demand response, demand-side resources, and energy-efficiency resources.
(5) Deployment of 'smart' technologies (real-time, automated, interactive technologies that optimize the physical operation of appliances and consumer devices) for metering, communications concerning grid operations and status, and distribution automation.
(6) Integration of 'smart' appliances and consumer devices.
(7) Deployment and integration of advanced electricity storage and peak-shaving technologies, including plug-in electric and hybrid electric vehicles, and thermal storage air conditioning.
(8) Provision to consumers of timely information and control options.
(9) Development of standards for communication and interoperability of appliances and equipment connected to the electric grid, including the infrastructure serving the grid.
(10) Identification and lowering of unreasonable or unnecessary barriers to adoption of smart grid technologies, practices, and services.

Solar and wind energy have to be produced where the sun shines and winds blow. Such locations are often distant from where the electricity is needed.

Thus, the energy, in one form or another has to be transmitted to where it is needed. This has created a major challenge to the transformation from fossil fuels to renewables.

> In reality, there is no single U.S. grid. There are three – one in the West, one in the East and one in Texas – that only connect at a few points and share little power between them. Those grids are further divided into a patchwork of operators with competing interests. That makes it hard to build the long-distance power lines needed to transport wind and solar nationwide. America's fragmented electric grid, which was largely built to accommodate coal and gas plants, is becoming a major obstacle to efforts to fight climate change.
>
> **(Popovich & Plumer, 2023)**

Innovations in Oversight

In contrast with earlier chapters, I will briefly summarize innovations that created oversight capabilities in anticipation of environmental and climate challenges. We have been better at this than is often assumed, although the necessary programs and activities have often faced difficulties in gaining Congressional approval and resources.

United States Weather Bureau (1890)

> In 1849, the Smithsonian Institution supplied weather instruments to telegraph companies and established an extensive observation network. Observations were submitted by telegraph to the Smithsonian, where weather maps were created. By the end of 1849, 150 volunteers throughout the United States were reporting weather observations to the Smithsonian regularly. By 1860, 500 stations were furnishing daily telegraphic weather reports to the *Washington Evening Star*, and as the network grew, other existing systems were gradually absorbed, including several state weather services.
>
> **(USWB, 2020)**

The ability to observe and display simultaneously observed weather data, through the use of the telegraph, quickly led to initial efforts toward the next logical advancement, the forecasting of weather. However, the ability to observe and forecast weather over much of the country, required considerable structure and organization, which could be provided through a government agency.

The weather service is first identified as a civilian agency in 1890 when Congress, at the request of President Benjamin Harrison, passed an act transferring the meteorological responsibilities of the Signal Service to the newly created U.S. Weather Bureau in the Department of Agriculture.

The bureau was renamed the National Weather Service when it became part of NOAA in 1970.

National Oceanic and Atmospheric Administration (NOAA) (1970)

In 1807, President Thomas Jefferson founded the US Coast and Geodetic Survey (as the Survey of the Coast) to provide nautical charts to the maritime community for safe passage into American ports and along our extensive coastline. The Weather Bureau was founded 1870 and, one year later, the US Commission of Fish and Fisheries was founded. Individually, these organizations were America's first physical science agency, America's first agency dedicated specifically to the atmospheric sciences, and America's first conservation agency.

> The cultures of scientific accuracy and precision, service to protect life and property, and stewardship of resources of these three agencies were brought together (by President Nixon) in 1970 with the establishment of NOAA, an agency within the Department of Commerce.
>
> **(NOAA, 2020)**

NOAA bills itself as "America's environmental intelligence agency."

NOAA has had a few troubles lately, ranging from its disputing of President Trump's personal weather forecast to his conflicts with the agency's executive leadership. For example, Trump replaced the agency's chief scientist with an individual who denies the reality of climate change (Flavelle & Friedman, 2020).

Environmental Protection Agency (EPA) (1970)

The American conversation about protecting the environment began in the 1960s. Rachel Carson had published her attack on the indiscriminate use of pesticides, *Silent Spring*, in 1962. Concern about air and water pollution had spread in the wake of disasters. An offshore oil rig in California fouled beaches with millions of gallons of spilled oil. Near Cleveland, Ohio, the Cuyahoga River, choking with chemical contaminants, had spontaneously burst into flames. Astronauts had begun photographing the Earth from space, heightening awareness that the Earth's resources are finite.

> In early 1970, as a result of heightened public concerns about deteriorating city air, natural areas littered with debris, and urban water supplies contaminated with dangerous impurities, President Richard Nixon presented the House and Senate a groundbreaking message on the environment. He created a council to consider how to organize federal government programs designed to reduce pollution, so that those programs could efficiently address the goals laid out in his message on the environment. Following the council's recommendations, the president sent to Congress a plan to consolidate many environmental responsibilities of the federal government under one agency, a new Environmental Protection Agency.
>
> **(EPA, 2020)**

The Trump administration has been working to reverse many of the EPA's accomplishments.

> The bulk of the rollbacks identified by the *Times* have been carried out by the Environmental Protection Agency, which has weakened Obama-era limits on planet-warming carbon dioxide emissions from power plants and from cars and trucks; removed protections from more than half the nation's wetlands; and withdrawn the legal justification for restricting mercury emissions from power plants. At the same time, the Interior Department has worked to open up more land for oil and gas leasing by limiting wildlife protections and weakening environmental requirements for projects.
>
> **(Popovich et al., 2020)**

Corporate Average Fuel Economy (CAFE) Standards (1975)

Congress first established Corporate Average Fuel Economy (CAFE) standards in 1975, principally in response to the 1973 oil embargo. These standards were intended to roughly double the average fuel economy of the new car fleet within 20 years. These standards were enacted under President Nixon and are administered by the National Highway Traffic and Safety Administration (NHSTA) within the Department of Transportation.

> The CAFE standards not only improve energy efficiency of the Nation's fleet, but also:
>
> - Reduce our petroleum consumption
> - Increase the availability of alternative fuel vehicles
> - Promote the advancement of innovative technologies
> - Lower greenhouse gas emissions, both helping to mitigate climate change and improve air quality
>
> NHTSA's standards since 1978 have saved (and will continue to save) many billions of gallons of fuel for American drivers.

(DOT, 2020)

It is interesting how policies can sometimes interact. The federal government and state of California have offered significant incentives for consumers to purchase battery electric vehicles (BEVs). Working with General Motors, we undertook a study to project market adoption both during and after government incentives (Liu, Rouse & Hanawalt, 2018). We found that sustaining the market after the BEV incentives ended would require substantial company investments.

In the process of this study, we learned that the incentives were luring customers away from high-fuel efficiency internal combustion (IC) vehicles. As a consequence, in order to meet CAFE targets, automobile manufacturers were lowering prices on IC vehicles to increase sales volumes. They were actually selling these vehicles at a significant loss per vehicle. Companies had to increase sales of large SUVs and pickup trucks to make up for these losses.

Thus, the BEV incentive policies and the CAFE policies were working against each other. To make matters worse, as later discussed, we assessed whether the BEVs were helping the environment. If the electricity used to charge the BEVs was from coal-fired power plants, there was no environmental benefit due to moving from IC vehicles to BEVs. The interactions of policies can be rather subtle and complicated.

Intergovernmental Panel on Climate Change (1988)

The United Nations Environment Program (UNEP) and the World Meteorological Organization (WMO) established the Intergovernmental Panel on Climate Change (IPCC) in 1988. Its assignment was

> to prepare a comprehensive review and recommendations with respect to the state of knowledge of the science of climate change; the social and economic impact of climate change, and potential response strategies and elements for inclusion in a possible future international convention on climate.

(IPCC, 2020)

The IPCC has

> had five assessment cycles and delivered five Assessment Reports, the most comprehensive scientific reports about climate change produced world-wide. In 2007, the IPCC and U.S. Vice-President Al Gore were jointly awarded the Nobel Peace Prize 'for their efforts to build up and disseminate greater knowledge about man-made climate change, and to lay the foundations for the measures that are needed to counteract such change.

(IPCC, 2020)

The US was a major contributor of funds to IPCC efforts until this commitment was ended in 2017 (Ekwurzel, 2017). Both President Reagan (1980–1988) and President Bush (1988–1992) supported addressing climate change and its impacts. John McCain, running for President in 2008, supported this as well. More recently, the fossil fuel industry, with President Trump as chief cheerleader, has invested enormous sums trying to debunk science and convince people that either climate change is a hoax, or that the economic investments needed to address it would be overwhelming (Davenport & Lipton, 2017).

EXPLOITATION OF ENERGY AND CLIMATE

The enormous growth in this industry has resulted in a range of exploitations, summarized in Table 7.1. Exploitation via "externalities" concerns societal impacts for which the extraction industry, utility generators, and service providers are not accountable. Exploiters focus on maximizing efficiency and profits at the expense of environment, health, and safety. A human-centered society creates mechanisms to counter these tendencies.

It is useful to differentiate the extraction of energy from its conversion to, for example, provide propulsion to vehicles. Extraction has environmental impacts such as methane from oil drilling and wastewater from fracking. However, the conversion of coal to electricity and the conversion of gas to vehicle propulsion have much greater CO_2 impacts.

Exploiters, primarily to maximize profits at the expense of the environment and health, include Big Oil – Exxon Mobil, Shell, Chevron, BP, et al. with annual revenues in excess of $1 trillion. These companies produce the fossil fuels we consume, currently 81% of our energy consumption. The remaining 19% are from renewable sources, including nuclear (Penn State, 2019). Renewables are up to 20% in 2023 (Wiatros-Motyka, 2023).

Another key player is OPEC, the Organization of the Petroleum Exporting Countries, an organization enabling the cooperation of leading oil-producing countries to influence the global oil market and maximize profit. CFR (2023) provides a year-by-year summary of US imports of foreign energy sources and related issues.

Countries that directly subsidize their populations from fossil fuel revenues (Yergin, 2020), including, rank ordered by per capita subsidy,

TABLE 7.1

Innovation and Exploitation in Energy and Climate

Innovations	Coal, oil, gas, and renewables.
Financial exploitation	Monopoly pricing and depressed wages.
Physical exploitation	Carbon and methane emissions and air pollution.
Psychological exploitation	Misinformation, disinformation, bad decisions, and needless worry.
Mitigating exploitation	Regulations, anti-trust laws, and externality taxes.

Qatar ($6,000), Saudi Arabia ($3,395), Russia ($2,334), United States ($2,177), China ($1,652), South Korea ($1,441), Canada ($1,283), Australia ($1,259), and Japan ($1,2490). The total is equivalent to 3.8% of global GDP per year (*The Guardian*, 2015).

Environmental Impacts

Greenhouse gas emissions by source include CO_2 73%, and methane 11% (CSS, 2022). There are substantial methane leaks from natural gas operations (EIA, 2023; UNEP, 2020). Fracking can negatively impact air and water quality in fracked areas. (Horton, 2023). Thus, extraction, not just conversion, impacts the environment significantly.

People's behaviors are also a determinant. "Impacts of natural disasters are determined by behaviors and practices embedded in society. Some measures to mitigate risk, such as floodwalls, subsidized insurance, and disaster relief, can increase it by encouraging more intensive development in risk" (*Economist*, 2023b).

Other behaviors include buying trucks and SUVs. Not only are the profit margins attractive to the vehicle manufacturers, but the convenience of avoiding CAFE requirements on such vehicles enables selling less efficient vehicles. As Van Dam (2023) points out, station wagons that used to be classified as automobiles are now classified as trucks and exempt from CAFE.

Superyachts provide a rather compelling example of exploitation.

> Owning or operating a superyacht is probably the most harmful thing an individual can do to the climate. If we're serious about avoiding climate chaos, we need to tax, or at the very least shame, these resource-hoarding behemoths out of existence. In fact, taking on the carbon aristocracy, and their most emissions-intensive modes of travel and leisure, may be the best chance we have to boost our collective "climate morale" and increase our appetite for personal sacrifice – from individual behavior changes to sweeping policy mandates.

> **(Fassler, 2023)**

Krugman suggests even greater significance.

> When rich people can afford to buy and operate big yachts, they do. Indeed, yachts are a highly visible indicator of inequality, the concentration of

income and wealth in the hands of the few. The Gilded Age was marked by a proliferation of ever bigger, ever more elaborately furnished yachts; when J.P. Morgan built a large steam yacht, its 1898 launch was featured in the *New York Times*.

(**Krugman, 2023**)

This is far from human-centered practice.

RESPONSES TO EXPLOITATION

An integrated response to mitigate exploitation is more likely to be enacted rather than piecemeal pieces of legislation having to overcome separate battles. Hence, I propose the following mitigation agenda.

Industry Resistance

Industries have demonstrated resistance to change. For example, President Biden's push to disclose climate risks has encountered a wall of industry resistance (Mufson, 2023). The increasing frequency of storms, floods, and fires has weakened the resistance to admit to the need to address climate change.

Industries' approach to shedding assets has included some questionable practices. Sales of foreign assets to local investors often result in health and safety programs being ignored or curtailed (Chason, 2023). Some companies are isolating dirty steelmaking-coal operations from the cleaner businesses of mining metals and minerals, without losing profits from coal. The idea is to squeeze as much profit from coal until it has run its course (*Economist*, 2023a).

Stopping coal production has turned out to be more difficult than politicians imagined, especially in the developing world.

All this points to a fundamental problem of relying on finance to limit fossil fuels: it does not target the demand for them. For as long as demand is high, people can make a profit from investing in coal – and someone, somewhere will seek to do so.

(*Economist,* **2023c**)

Mitigation Agenda

Legislation may be needed to address monopolistic activities, although the Department of Justice has the necessary tools. This is complicated by natural gas, electricity companies, and other utility companies being "natural monopolies." The capital costs to enter the industry are high, and it is very difficult to attract customers away from incumbent providers. The Department of Justice has nevertheless been involved in the industry.

Enron tried to corner the commodity natural gas market. To manage the great risks in this market, Enron started to look more like a finance company than an energy company (Penney, 2023). For example, they increased financial investments in gas turbines for the utilities that were buying their gas. As they grew, the use of accounting loopholes, special purpose entities, and poor financial reporting enabled the company to hide billions of dollars in debt from failed deals and projects. Enron declared bankruptcy in 2001.

The resulting scandal led to the prosecution of key executives by the Department of Justice. New regulations and legislation were enacted to expand the accuracy of financial reporting for public companies. One piece of legislation, the Sarbanes–Oxley Act of 2002, increased penalties for destroying, altering, or fabricating records in federal investigations or for attempting to defraud shareholders.

Two decades later, the legacy of Enron's push for deregulation affected Texas' winter woes.

> Enron was never able to realize the goal of nationwide deregulation. The U.S. electricity system remains a patchwork of different regulatory systems across different states. Yet, the legacy of Enron's push lives on in Texas. The combination of the failing power grid and market forces have pushed the price of electricity into the thousands of dollars, leaving consumers facing astronomical bills for just a few days of service, and legislators facing pressure to act to help their constituents.
>
> **(Benke, 2021)**

Legislation is needed to address direct industry emissions, rather than emissions from vehicle use. Externality taxes, as discussed in earlier chapters, would be levied on companies and consumers. Thus, consumers would pay more for electricity generated by coal-fired plants, and producers would pay higher taxes on such revenues.

Legislation is also needed to address misinformation and disinformation about energy and climate. It might be difficult to ban misleading or outright erroneous company advertisements but, as with cigarettes, such advertisements could be required to include labels explaining the lack of evidence supporting the advertisement's claims.

Failure Management

I chronicle 18 well-known malfunctions of technologies, organizations, and society in *Failure Management* (Rouse, 2021). Four of these cases involved the energy industry:

- Three Mile Island (1979) – radiation release
- Chernobyl (1986) – radiation release
- Exxon Valdez (1989) – oil spill
- BP Deepwater Horizon (2010) – oil spill

Plokhy (2022) provides a more comprehensive review of nuclear-related accidents and disasters.

I outline a decision support framework that could have been applied to all 18 malfunctions to detect, diagnose, and remediate the failures. Legislation could require that energy companies adopt this framework, or equivalent, to manage failures. Some combination of EPA, FERC, and NRC could ensure that companies comply with this regulation.

Investment Tradeoffs

It is important to point out critical investment tradeoffs (*Economist*, 2023d, 2023e). Given limited resources, especially in developing countries, they

> could plough what little resources remain into the health-care system: dollars spent by clinics help control infectious diseases, and there is not much that development experts believe to be a better use of cash.
>
> But you could also spend the money constructing an electrical grid that is able to handle a switch to clean energy. In the long run this will mean less pollution, more productive farmland and fewer floods. Which is a wiser

use of the marginal dollar: alleviating acute poverty straight away or doing your country's bit to stop baking the planet?

Growth is the best way to lift people out of poverty and improve average living standards. But in the developing world, more growth still leads to more emissions.

(*Economist*, 2023e)

The tradeoff is between alleviating poverty now or investing in the means to provide a better future. Resolution of this tradeoff in a conundrum.

It gets more complicated.

The effect of global warming on the world's poorest people provides a compelling case. As the planet heats up, extreme events such as droughts, floods and storms are becoming more common and more severe. Many places are becoming less habitable. Over the coming decades many vulnerable farmers will find their crops failing more frequently. And as resources grow scarcer, more fighting will break out.

This pattern is no longer just a warning by activists. It is accepted by the mainstream to the point where fears of a surge in climate migration are fodder for the nativist right. Because people are understandably troubled by the idea of climate change forcing poor farmers to leave behind their ancestral lands, an important goal of adaptation spending is to help them stay.

(*Economist*, 2023e)

Racially minoritized groups, migrants, and Indigenous communities face a disproportionate burden of illness and mortality due to climate change in different contexts. The health community must urgently examine and repair the structural discrimination that drives the unequal impacts of climate change to achieve rapid and equitable action.

(**Deivanayagam et al., 2023**)

The bottom line tradeoff is between alleviating misery now versus avoiding future misery. We all face this tradeoff but certainly not to the extent of minoritized groups, migrants, and Indigenous communities. A human-centered society realizes they are facing this tradeoff and engages in a deep understanding and analysis of how best to resolve it.

TABLE 7.2

Selected US Government Agencies

Agency (Founding)	Agency Charter
EPA (1970)	The Environmental Protection Agency is an independent executive agency of the United States federal government tasked with environmental protection matters.
FERC (1977)	The Federal Energy Regulatory Commission is the United States federal agency that regulates the transmission and wholesale sale of electricity and natural gas in interstate commerce and regulates the transportation of oil by pipeline in interstate commerce.
IPCC (1988)	The Intergovernmental Panel on Climate Change is an intergovernmental body of the United Nations. Its job is to advance scientific knowledge about climate change caused by human activities. The World Meteorological Organization and the United Nations Environment Program established the IPCC.
NOAA (1970)	The National Oceanic and Atmospheric Administration is a Washington, DC-based scientific and regulatory agency within the United States Department of Commerce.
NRC (1975)	The Nuclear Regulatory Commission is an independent agency of the United States government tasked with protecting public health and safety related to nuclear energy.
NWS (1870)	The National Weather Service is an agency of the United States federal government that is tasked with providing weather forecasts, warnings of hazardous weather, and other weather-related products to organizations and the public for the purposes of protection, safety, and general information.

Role of Government

The charters of the government agencies involved in the mitigation agenda are summarized in Table 7.2. Business practice issues are considered by EPA, FERC, and NRC. EPA, NOAA, and NWS are concerned with weather and environmental impacts. IPCC addresses global issues.

CONCLUSIONS

The need for energy is constant and pervasive, as illustrated by several chapters in this book. Energy is a keystone in our economy. Yet our reliance on fossil fuels has led to dangerous exploitation of the environment and global warming. We have to stem the tide (MIT, 2015). This chapter has laid out the central elements of an integrated solution.

To supplement and complement the perspective I have provided in this chapter, we can call on luminaries John Doerr, Bill Gates, and Paul Hawken for their thought leadership. Their three 2021 books provide compelling prescriptions.

Doerr (2021) presents "a compelling 10-step plan to cut greenhouse gas emissions to net zero by 2050 that includes electrifying our energy grid to fixing our global food supply chain to capturing carbon from the air."

Gates (2021) "describes the areas in which technology is already helping to reduce emissions, where and how the current technology can be made to function more effectively, where breakthrough technologies are needed, and who is working on these essential innovations."

Hawken (2021) advocates

> initiatives that include but go well beyond solar, electric vehicles, and tree planting to include such solutions as the fifteen-minute city, bioregions, azolla fern, food localization, fire ecology, decommodification, forests as farms, and the number one solution for the world: electrifying everything.

All three agree that sustainability is achievable, as well as providing compelling opportunities for innovation and economic growth.

REFERENCES

Benke, G. (2021). Energy deregulation worsened the Texas crisis – And Enron is partly to blame. *Washington Post*, February 23.

CFR. (2023). *Oil Dependence and U.S. Foreign Policy: 1850–2022: Council on Foreign Relations*. Washington, DC: Council on Foreign Relations.

Chason, R. (2023). Big Oil is selling off its polluting assets – with unintended consequences. *Washington Post*, March 27.

CSS. (2022). *U.S. Energy System Factsheet* (Pub. No. CSS03-11). Ann Arbor, MI: Center for Sustainable Systems, University of Michigan.

Davenport, C., & Lipton, E. (2017). How GOP leaders came to view climate change as fake science. *New York Times*, June 3.

Deivanayagam, A.B., et al. (2023). Envisioning environmental equity: Climate change, health, and racial justice. *Lancet*, 402, 64–78.

Doerr, J. (2021). *Speed & Scale: An Action Plan for Solving Our Climate Crisis Now*. New York: Portfolio.

DOT. (2020). *Corporate Average Fuel Economy (CAFE) Standards*. https://www.transportation.gov/mission/sustainability/corporate-average-fuel-economy-cafe-standards.

Economist. (2023a).The tug-of-war between Glencore and Teck. *The Economist*, April 13.

Economist. (2023b). What to read to understand the biggest natural disasters. *The Economist*, April 14.

Economist. (2023c). The struggle to kill King Coal. *The Economist*, June 8.

Economist. (2023d). The choice between a poorer today and a hotter tomorrow. *The Economist*, June 27.

Economist. (2023e). How misfiring environmentalism risks harming the world's poor: The trade-off between development and climate change is impossible to avoid. *The Economist*, June 29.

EIA. (2023). *Natural Gas and the Environment*. Washington, DC: US Energy Information Administration.

Ekwurzel, B. (2017). US Abandons global science leadership, Zeroes out IPCC funding. *Common Dreams*, August 9.

EPA. (2020). *The Origins of the EPA*. https://www.epa.gov/history/origins-epa.

Fassler, J. (2023). The superyachts of billionaires are starting to look a lot like theft. *New York Times*, April 10.

Flavelle, C., & Friedman, L. (2020). As election nears, Trump makes a final push against climate science. *New York Times*, October 28.

Gates, B. (2021). *How to Avoid a Climate Disaster: The Solutions We Have and the Breakthroughs We Need*. New York: Vintage.

Grubler, A. (2012). Grand designs: Historical patterns and future scenarios of energy technological change. In: A. Grubler et al., Eds., *The Global Energy Assessment* (Chapter 24). Cambridge: Cambridge University Press.

Guardian. (2015). G20 countries pay over $1,000 per citizen in fossil fuel subsidies, says IMF. *The Guardian*, August 4.

Hawken, P. (2021). *Regeneration: Ending the Climate Crisis in One Generation*. New York: Penguin.

Horton, M. (2023). How does fracking affect the environment? Fracking can negatively impact air and water quality in fracked areas. https://www.investopedia.com/. April 17.

IPCC. (2020). *The History of IPCC*. https://www.ipcc.ch/about/history/.

Krugman, P. (2023). Inequality ahoy! On the meaning of the superyacht. *New York Times*, April 11.

Liu, C., Rouse, W.B., & Hanawalt, E. (2018). Adoption of powertrain technologies in automobiles: A system dynamics model of technology diffusion in the American market. *IEEE Transactions on Vehicular Technology*, 67 (7), 5621–5634.

MIT. (2015). *A Plan for Action on Climate Change*. Cambridge, MA: Massachusetts Institute of Technology.

Mufson, S. (2023). Biden's push to disclose climate risks hits wall of industry resistance. *Washington Post*, May 2.

NAP. (2023). *Laying the Foundation for New and Advanced Nuclear Reactors in the United States (2023)*. Washington, DC: National Academies Press.

Newell, R.G. (2011). *The Energy Innovation System: A Historical Perspective*. Cambridge, MA: National Bureau of Economic Research.

NOAA. (2020). *Our History.* https://www.noaa.gov/our-history.

Penn State. (2019). *Energy Production and Consumption in the United States.* State College, PA: Pennsylvania State University, College of Earth & Mineral Sciences. https://www.e-education.psu.edu/ebf301/.

Penney, E. (2023). Enron after all: A history of our broken energy paradigm. *American Affairs*, February 20.

Plokhy, S. (2022). *Atoms and Ashes: A Global History of Nuclear Disasters.* New York: Norton.

Popovich, N., Albeck-Ripka, L., & Pierre-Louis, K. (2020). The Trump administration is reversing more than 100 environmental rules. *New York Times*, November 10.

Popovich, N., & Plumer, B. (2023). Why the US electric grid isn't ready for the energy transition. *New York Times*, June 13.

Power. (2022). History of power: The evolution of the electric generation industry. *Power Magazine*, October 1.

Puko, T. (2023). This power plant offers a peak into the future. *Washington Post*, May 1.

Rouse, W.B. (2021). *Failure Management: Malfunctions of Technologies, Organizations, and Society.* Oxford: Oxford University Press.

UNEP. (2020). Homing in on methane emissions from the oil and gas industry. *UNEP News.* https://www.unep.org/. May 8.

USWB. (2020). History of the National Weather Service. https://www.weather.gov/timeline.

Van Dam, A. (2023). The real reason trucks have taken over US roadways. *Washington Post*, April 7.

Wiatros-Motyka, M. (2023). Global electricity review 2023. *Ember*, April 12.

Yergin, D. (2020). *The New Map: Energy, Climate, and the Clash of Nations.* New York: Penguin.

8

Creating the Balance

Chapters 2–7 outlined an innovation landscape over the past couple of centuries. Technological innovation has driven economic growth. The innovators have prospered but huge segments of our population have been exploited – financially, physically, and psychologically. In this final chapter, I integrate the many findings from earlier chapters into an exploitation landscape. I then consider what might be our collective responses to this landscape and how these responses can enable a human-centered society.

EXPLOITATION LANDSCAPE

Table 8.1 summarizes the exploitation landscape across the five ecosystems I have addressed. The top row summarizes the innovations in these five ecosystems. I have written extensively on these innovations, initially some time ago (Rouse, 1996, 1998, 2001) and also quite recently (Rouse, 2015, 2019, 2022, 2023, 2024). The five columns in this table are populated with findings discussed in Chapters 3–7.

Financial Exploitation

Monopoly pricing results in profits that are exorbitant. Depressed wages can also inflate profits. Customers may realize that they are paying too much, but feel "locked in" to particular offerings, with the costs of change being perceived as too high. Waste, fraud, and abuse are more likely in markets with little or no competition.

DOI: 10.4324/9781003462361-8

TABLE 8.1

Innovation Landscape for Five Ecosystems

	Domain				
Innovations	**Transportation and Defense**	**Computers and Communications**	**Internet and social Media**	**Health and Wellness**	**Energy and Climate**
Innovations	Ships Railroads Automobiles Airplanes	Mainframes Minicomputers Microcomputers Digital devices	ARPANET TCP/IP World wide web Browsers	Public Health Vaccines Genomics Telehealth	Coal Oil Gas Renewables
Financial exploitation	Monopoly pricing Depressed wages Waste, fraud, and abuse	Vendor lock-In High frequency trading cryptocurrency	Monopoly pricing Vendor lock-In	Monopoly pricing Depressed wages Waste, fraud, and abuse	Monopoly pricing Depressed wages
Physical exploitation	Air pollution Noise pollution Carbon emissions Accident injuries	Server emissions Toxic waste Electronics trash	Server emissions Outcomes of bad info and advice Outrage injuries	Avoidable disease Failed treatment Early death	Carbon and methane emissions Air pollution
Psychological Exploitation	Traffic stress Traveling stress Needless worry	Learning curves Failed connections Inactive lifestyles	Misinformation Disinformation Anger, fear, and depression	False advertising Misinformation Disinformation	Misinformation Disinformation Bad decisions Needless worry
Mitigating Exploitation	Regulations, anti-trust laws Externality taxes	Regulations, anti-trust laws Externality taxes	Regulations, anti-trust laws Media laws Externality taxes	Regulations, anti-trust laws Advertising laws Externality taxes	Regulations, anti-trust laws Externality taxes

Defense contractors typically have monopoly positions on platforms, e.g., F-35 fighter aircraft. While the government controls profit margins, it is much more difficult to control costs incurred, and padding can be easy to conceal. Much of healthcare operates with a fee-for-service business model. Unnecessary and repeated tests and procedures are common. The US is the poster child for the resulting excess costs, unfortunately often with poor results.

Pharmaceutical companies manipulate the drug approval and patenting system to avoid sharing critical data and sustain high prices. Consequently, drugs in the US are far more expensive than in other countries. Pharma companies aggressively lobby to hinder any attempts to address this exploitation.

Physical Exploitation

Physical exploitation often results from "externalities" of pollution, emissions, trash, accidents, and deaths. These are termed externalities because the producers of these outcomes are not liable for the costs of remediating them. Physical harm can also result from bad advice, ranging from misinformation to disinformation. This can lead to a lack of treatments, incorrect treatments, poor outcomes, and sometimes death.

Society is forced to pay the costs of these externalities for direct cleanup, disaster recovery, and health consequences. Innovators strongly resist attempts to decrease these outcomes or to pay for them. Taxpayers have to shoulder the costs of these exploitations.

Psychological Exploitation

Psychological exploitation includes various forms of stress and worry. Misinformation and disinformation can lead to anger, fear, and depression. Self-images may become distorted and personal aspirations delusional. Learning curves may be hindered or thwarted. Bad decisions can result such as experienced by recent decisions to avoid vaccines.

Figure 8.1 summarizes these findings in terms of financial, physical, and psychological exploitation, as well as facilitating factors.

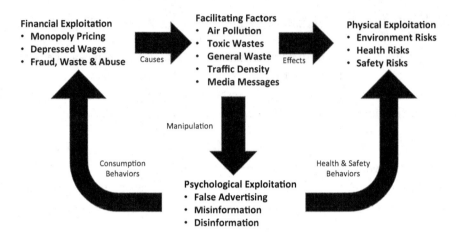

FIGURE 8.1
Dynamics of exploitation

MITIGATING EXPLOITATION

The bottom row of Table 8.1 provides a summary of potential mitigations. The possibilities include:

- Anti-trust laws as administrated by the Federal Trade Commission and the Department of Justice
- Broadcast media laws as administered by the Federal Communications Commission
- Advertising laws as administrated by the Federal Trade Commission
- Taxes on "externalities" – innovators are taxed to compensate – require Congressional actions, as well as the involvement of the other agencies discussed below

Table 8.2 provides a brief summary of landmark anti-trust cases. The Microsoft settlement was motivated by the dominance of MS Windows and MS Office in general and, in particular, MS Explorer being the only browser on MS Windows. The settlement required Microsoft to share its application programming interfaces with third-party companies.

The timeliness of these types of mitigations is an issue, as illustrated by the three- to nine-year delays in Table 8.2. The US legal system allows

TABLE 8.2

Landmark Antitrust Cases

Company	Case Filed	Case Decided	Outcome
Standard Oil Trust	1906	1911	Breakup
US Steel	1911	1920	No Breakup
AT&T	1974	1982	Breakup
Microsoft	1998	2001	Settlement

for extended delays and appeals, as evidenced by the highly publicized legal antics of a recent US president. This process has important merits but needs to be streamlined.

Externalities are consequences created or enabled by companies, for which they have no legal responsibilities. Examples include pollution, e.g., industrial effluents; hazardous waste, e.g., chemicals employed to produce semiconductors; and environmental damage, e.g., discarded electronics in landfills. Carbon and methane emissions contribute to storms, fires, and floods, as well as sickness and disease over time.

Why are companies able to avoid responsibility for such consequences? They lobby Congress, as well as provide ample political contributions, to shield these benefactors from these responsibilities. If elections were government-funded, as practiced by other OECD countries, these phenomena could be thwarted.

There is another level of externalities. Cars and trucks create traffic, leading to accidents, injuries, and deaths. Guns also lead to injuries and deaths. Manufacturers of these products argue that they cannot be blamed for how customers use their products. Automobile manufacturers are getting better at creating ways to detect alcohol-impaired drivers to thwart drunken driving. Gun manufacturers, in contrast, have been more creative in promoting the misuse of assault weapons (Frankel et al., 2023).

We have laws and regulations to prevent pharmaceutical companies from harming the users of their drugs. This process has enormous flaws. OxyContin entered the market in 1996 when the FDA approved its original label, which stated that addiction was "very rare" if opioids were legitimately used in the management of pain. Their evidence was a couple of sentences in a letter to the editor of the *New England Journal of Medicine*.

Their aggressive marketing and outright lying about the risks of OxyContin have resulted in over one million deaths from overdoses.

Purdue Pharma pleaded guilty to federal criminal charges twice, in 2007 and in 2020, based on deceptive marketing that downplayed the risk. The company was fined $2 billion, or roughly $2,000 per death. Thus, full resolution took 24 years, while enormous numbers of people were dying.

MITIGATION STRATEGIES

Should we try to engender another Progressive Era to limit exploitations to fair returns on investments by the innovators? We could make the exploiters directly pay for their exploitation, for example, by taxing them for the costs to remediate emissions, pollution, and toxic waste. This might motivate these firms to function more like "circular economies," such that there are no effluents, waste, etc. Firms in the same markets might scale up and share small successes to broader implementation across their markets.

Levying taxes so the government can pay for mitigation could be an overarching strategy. The corporate tax rates would be higher for exploiters, contingent on the magnitude of the consequences of exploitation. The current 21% corporate tax rate could be maintained for non-exploiters, increasing to 50% to 70% for the most grievous exploiters. The increased revenues would go into a Mitigation Trust Fund, much in the ways the Medicare and Social Security tax revenues are managed.

Congress would be responsible for determining appropriate tax rates and the criteria whereby they would be applied. This would be very contentious and involve thousands of lobbyists trying to preempt such legislation, and perhaps billions of dollars in campaign contributions intended to sway the decisions of legislators. Fortunately there are government agencies that can inform this process. Here are two examples.

The Food and Drug Administration (FDA), an agency of the Department of Health and Human Services, must approve new drugs and biological products for people before they are marketed in interstate commerce. This means that a company must demonstrate that its drug or biological product is safe and effective for the intended use and that it can manufacture the product to federal quality standards.

Pharmaceutical companies have been very successful in neutering these regulations (Abramson, 2022). They avoid providing data on trials, claiming that such information is proprietary. Instead, they verbally tell the FDA about their success – with little or no empirical evidence. Then, primarily via aggressive TV ads, they convince the American public that they need these ineffective and expensive drugs – forever. Their intent is to lock-in patients, not cure their diseases. Pure exploitation.

With regard to environmental protection, the Health Resources and Services Administration (HRSA), also an agency of the Department of Health and Human Services, performs environmental assessments under the National Environmental Policy Act. This results in a concise public document that provides sufficient evidence and analysis for determining whether HRSA should issue a finding of no significant environmental impact or prepare an Environmental Impact Statement. Industries are quite creative in justifying the no-impact finding.

Certification, permitting, etc. can mitigate exploitation but tend to be very time-consuming, usually involving years and sometimes decades. Companies often take their chances in the courts, which further slows everything down. Rather than being human-centered, these sequences of hurdles, and how they are circumvented, increase the likelihood of exploitation, especially its duration.

Other major hurdles can involve First Amendment issues. The First Amendment of the US Constitution protects freedom of speech. The US Supreme Court has consistently ruled that lying is protected (Rosenberg, 2021) from criminal prosecution. Civil prosecution is feasible but can take a long time and be expensive. Deep pockets may bring it back to the Supreme Court for adjudication.

False advertising is untrue or misleading information provided to consumers to get them to buy something, or at least pay attention to market offerings. Those who make and sell products are supposed to honestly represent their products, services, and prices. However, carefully designed advertisements can cause consumers to have perceptions that are unfounded.

For example, TV ads for pharmaceuticals tend to show happy people participating in enjoyable activities on a beautiful day. The truth may be that the drug in question benefits 5% of the people taking it and yields a 6–8% improvement in health outcomes. However, this is not false advertising because companies never claim specific improvements.

Further, there are explicit statements of possible negative side effects. My favorite is, "May lead to strong suicidal thoughts, and deep depression. If this is not normal for you, contact your physician." This is absolutely true, but the people in the ad look so happy and are enjoying themselves. Many patients will ask their physicians about this drug. If it was OxyContin, these patients may now be dead.

This leads to the question of who is responsible. The patients were not forced to consume the drugs. Drivers were not forced to drive recklessly under the influence of alcohol. Gun owners who choose to shoot people, including young schoolchildren, were not forced to use their guns in this manner. The designers and manufacturers of these drugs, vehicles, and guns did not directly contribute to these unfortunate outcomes. Yet perhaps they did.

Who is responsible for mitigating these types of exploitation? Should individualistic entrepreneurs and innovators be expected to address these needs? Or should a collectivist society, using laws, regulations, and incentives take the lead in identifying and mitigating exploitation? Different societies address this question in varying ways, e.g., Scandinavian countries vs. the US.

A central issue in this debate is the extent to which economic growth is driven by market forces or government planning. As summarized in Chapter 1, Hayek and Friedman argue that market forces determine everything and government should stay out of the way. Keynes and Polanyi counter that market forces are important, but sometimes result in disruptive outcomes, like discrimination and unemployment, that entrepreneurs and innovators are unwilling to address. The government needs to stabilize situations such as the Great Depression (1929–39) and the Great Recession (2007–2009).

Once disruptive outcomes become sufficiently obvious, the electorate responds and developments such as the Progressive Era emerge. We need to be more proactive to short-circuit such inefficient processes. However, we are plagued by American tendencies, as once famously observed by Winston Churchill, "Americans will always do the right thing, only after they have tried everything else."

A good approach to productively address remediations involves developing an agreed-upon set of rules. Ostrom's rules for the "commons" are a great example (Ostrom, 2015; Williams, 2018). The commons include elements of society that are collectively owned and used by many. The governance of natural resources is her primary concern, including meadows and forests, irrigation communities and other water rights, and fisheries.

1. Commons need to have clearly defined boundaries. In particular, who is entitled to access to what? Unless there's a specified community of benefit, it becomes a free-for-all all, and that's not how commons work.
2. Rules should fit local circumstances. There is no one-size-fits-all approach to common resource management. Rules should be dictated by local people and local ecological needs.
3. Participatory decision-making is vital. There are all kinds of ways to make it happen, but people will be more likely to follow the rules if they have a hand in writing them. Involve as many people as possible in decision-making.
4. Commons must be monitored. Once rules have been set, communities need a way of checking that people are keeping them. Commons don't run on goodwill but on accountability.
5. Sanctions for those who abuse the commons should be graduated. Ostrom observed that the commons that worked best didn't just ban people who broke the rules. That tended to create resentment. Instead, they had systems of warnings and fines, as well as informal reputational consequences in the community.
6. Conflict resolution should be easily accessible. When issues come up, resolving them should be informal, cheap, and straightforward. That means that anyone can take their problems for mediation, and nobody is shut out. Problems are solved rather than ignoring them because nobody wants to pay legal fees.
7. Commons need the right to organize. Your commons rules won't count for anything if a higher local authority doesn't recognize them as legitimate.
8. Commons work best when nested within larger networks. Some things can be managed locally, but some might need wider regional cooperation – for example an irrigation network might depend on a river that others also draw on upstream.

These guidelines make great sense for natural resources. How might they apply to health and education? Various pieces of the health and education ecosystems are owned by public and private constituencies. Yet the overall ecosystems are owned by everybody. Clearly the translation of Ostrom's principles to the contexts pursued here will require some deep thinking.

RESEARCH ROADMAP

Success in all of these endeavors depends on understanding and affecting behavioral and social phenomena. Figure 8.2 summarizes an initial roadmap for achieving these ends.

A recent initiative focused on the opioid epidemic provides a good illustration (Tolk et al., 2023). The focus was on social, rather than medical, interventions to address the opioid crisis. We developed an agent-based model of Washington, DC, with 700,000 agents – the population of DC. Data came from each of the eight wards in the city, supplemented with national data. Thus, each agent in the model had an address, gender, age, family membership, school district, etc.

A detailed review of 250 medical research articles on substance abuse, enabled the development of a state-based model of people in one of five states: at risk of addiction, already addicted, overdosed, recovered, and dead. Many papers in the 250-article corpus reported on how recovered addicts can be quite effective in getting current addicts to pursue recovery. Thus, we focused on getting addicts connected to recovered individuals in their neighborhoods. Of course, this connection was just computational.

We simulated the interactions of agents in Washington, DC, and projected the incidence of opioid abuse, overdoses, and deaths in each of the eight wards, which differ hugely in terms of determinants of health. Our incident projections for each of the eight wards were comparable to actual measurements. We also projected the improvements due to getting addicts connected to recovered individuals in this neighborhood.

The coronavirus pandemic provided an unfortunate opportunity to test our hypothesis of the impacts of social connections. We developed projections, assuming that everyone in DC was socially isolated. Actual incidents of overdoses and deaths increased substantially. Our model's projections were aligned with these measured outcomes. Thus, we know that social networks can play important roles in mitigating crises.

There is a range of technology trends related to the projections in the roadmap in Figure 8.2 (NAP, 2021; Rouse & Spohrer, 2018; Tegmark, 2017). Interoperability, augmented intelligence, and service coordination are organizational aspirations, with a range of behavioral and social components. Technology investments and innovations will be key enablers

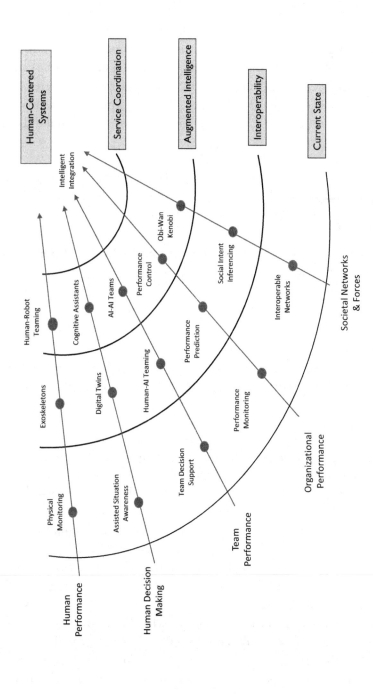

FIGURE 8.2

Roadmap for understanding behavioral and social phenomena

of these outcomes. Of course, opportunities for exploitation will need to be assessed and managed as well.

The media is awash in projections of the impacts of ChatGPT. These projections range from the mass replacement of human workers to the intelligent augmentation of these humans. I recently tested it with a range of questions about economics and society. Several of its answers were quite cogent. In a couple of cases, it responded, "I do not know how to answer that question." As I noted in Chapter 5, I found it reassuring that it did not just wing it.

CHALLENGES

What is the likely evolution toward a human-centered society? Here are a few indications that we have quite a ways to go:

- Over one million US deaths from opioid abuse
- Over one million US deaths from the Covid-19 pandemic, eight times higher for unvaccinated
- 38,000 annual automobile crash fatalities in US, 30% due to alcohol
- 40,000 annual fatalities due to gun violence in US, 50% due to suicide

Here are the consequences.

> Life expectancy in America has dropped for a nearly unprecedented second year in a row – down to 76 years. While countries all over the world saw life expectancy rebound during the second year of the pandemic after the arrival of vaccines, the U.S. did not.
>
> **(Simmons-Duffin, 2023)**

Further, these types of deaths disproportionately occur among people who are economically and socially challenged. They are exploited in the sense that they do not have access to health, education, and social services that most of us take for granted. We know what to do to mitigate these inequities, but seemingly do not have the will and resources to do it.

Who will enable the changes associated with creating a human-centered society? Many change agents have been working diligently for many decades. Human-centered design has long been taught in college majors in engineering, computer science, and psychology. These offerings need to be expanded to include business, medicine, law, and policy. Elements of this philosophy need to be integrated into K-12 civics classes.

Historically human-centered design courses have focused on aircraft cockpits, automobile dashboards, appliances, and other devices humans operate (Norman, 2013). The profound and fundamental guidance provided by this and other classics is essential to safe and useful equipment and devices. More recently, Norman (2023) has broadened this perspective to align with the landscape I have articulated here.

We need to move the goalposts. The overarching goal is human-centered systems for health, education, energy, and information services. Succinctly put, the goal is a human-centered society. Thus, the human-centered systems movement aspires to enhance human abilities, overcome human limitations, and foster human acceptance across all aspects of social interactions and society.

Beyond education, albeit expanded, community engagement needs to provide many agents of change. This includes parent-teacher organizations, sports clubs, church groups, block or neighborhood associations, 4-H clubs, and many others. Churches can play a particularly important role as human-centered design aligns with many theologies.

Advocacy groups such as the American Civil Liberties Union, American Library Association, Planned Parenthood, United Farm Workers, United States Chamber of Commerce, and many others can be important stakeholders in advocating the human-centered systems movement. We are seeking the hearts and minds of stakeholders, not so much their material resources.

The human-centered society movement will seek media coverage, broadly defined to include broadcast, entertainment, and social media. The human-centered story needs to be told and reinforced. Success stories, as well as unfortunate stories of failure, need to be communicated. These stories need to be packaged as personal, human stories, not statistics.

Committed leadership is the key to success. We need teachers, clergy, and political leaders who deeply understand the human-centered society movement and are committed to telling the stories, articulating support, and expanding the base of support. In my experience, few people find the goals of a human-centered society unappealing; they are more likely to

TABLE 8.3

Transparency vs. Accountability

		Accountability	
		Low	High
Transparency	**High**	Everybody knows what is happening but does not know what they should do	Everybody knows what is happening and feels responsible
	Low	Nobody knows what is happening and nobody feels responsible	No one is sure about what is happening but are prepared to be responsible

be skeptical of success. Strong, committed, and articulate leadership can transform these perceptions.

Table 8.3 depicts a central aspect of a human-centered society. We need both high transparency and high accountability to understand exploitation and feel empowered to address it. These outcomes are enabled by education, which has not been a strong suit in the US of late (Winchester, 2023). George Will suggests that mediocrity has, unfortunately, become our K-12 aspiration in the US (Will, 2023).

Transparency requires abilities to ascertain and understand financial, physical, and psychological exploitation. Social media has made this increasingly difficult. Accountability must include abilities to act, at least at the ballot box, but also in neighborhoods and communities. A human-centered movement needs engagement and empowerment, enabled by trust (McNutt & Crow, 2023).

CONCLUSIONS

Innovation is often driven by the desire to exploit technologies and market opportunities. These motivations are important, but innovators often have strong tendencies to pursue extremes, creating monopolies, suppressing employees' incomes and working conditions, and ignoring environmental impacts. A human-centered society will not tolerate such exploitation. We need to create the social, political, and economic infrastructure to anticipate and mitigate exploitation, without undermining the fruits of innovation.

REFERENCES

Abramson, J. (2022). *Sickening: How Big Pharma Broke American Health Care and How We Can Repair It*. Boston: Mariner.

Frankel, T.C., Boburg, S., Dawsey, J., Parker, A., & Horton, A. (2023). How the AR-15 became a powerful, political cultural symbol in America. *Washington Post*, March 27.

McNutt, M., & Crow, M.M. (2023). Enhancing trust in science and democracy in an age of misinformation. *Issues in Science & Technology*, 39 (3), 18–20.

NAP. (2021). *Human-AI Teaming: State of the Art and Research Needs*. Washington, DC: National Academies Press.

Norman, D.A. (2013). *Design of Everyday Things*. New York: Basic Books.

Norman, D.A. (2023). *Design for a Better World: Meaningful, Sustainable, Humanity Centered*. Cambridge, MA: MIT Press.

Ostrom, E. (2015). *Governing the Commons: The Evolution of Institutions for Collective Action*. Cambridge: Cambridge University Press.

Rosenberg, I. (2021). *The Fight for Free Speech: Ten Cases that Define Our First Amendment Freedoms*. New York: New York University Press.

Rouse, W.B. (2015). *Modeling and Visualization of Complex Systems and Enterprises: Explorations of Physical, Human, Economic, and Social Phenomena*. New York: Wiley.

Rouse, W.B. (2019). *Computing Possible Futures: Model Based Explorations of "What If?"* Oxford: Oxford University Press.

Rouse, W.B. (2022). *Transforming Public-Private Ecosystems: Understanding and Enabling Innovation in Complex Systems*. Oxford: Oxford University Press.

Rouse, W.B. (2023). *Bigger Pictures for Innovation: Creating Solutions, Managing Enterprises & Influencing Policies*. Oxfordshire: Routledge.

Rouse, W.B. (2024). *Beyond Quick Fixes: Addressing the Complexity & Uncertainties of Contemporary Society*. Oxford: Oxford University Press.

Rouse, W.B., & Spohrer, J.C. (2018). Automating versus augmenting intelligence. *Journal of Enterprise Transformation*. https://doi.org/10.1080/19488289.2018.1424059.

Simmons-Duffin, S. (2023). Live free and die? The sad state of US life expectancy. *Health News from NPR*, March 25.

Tegmark, M. (2017). *Life 3.0: Being Human in the Age of Artificial Intelligence*. New York: Knopf.

Tolk, A., Rouse, W.B., Pires, B.S., Cline, J.C, Diallo, S.Y., Sybil, A., & Russell, S.A. (2023). Applicability of artificial societies to evaluate health care policies. *Simulation in Healthcare*. https://doi.org/10.1097/SIH.0000000000000718.

Will, G. (2023). Why K-12 education's alarming decline could be a dominant 2024 issue. *Washington Post*, June 28.

Williams, J. (2018). *Elinor Ostrom's 8 Rules for Managing the Commons*. https://earth-bound.report/2018/01/15/elinor-ostroms-8-rules-for-managing-the-commons/. Accessed 01/12/23.

Winchester, S. (2023). *Knowing What We Know: The Transmission of Knowledge from Ancient Wisdom to Modern Magic*. Sydney: HarperCollins.

Index

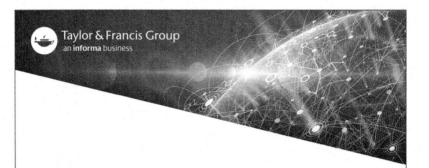

Printed in the United States
by Baker & Taylor Publisher Services